~~~MENT COOPERATION IRELAND

Visions OF THE FUTURE

Visions OF THE FUTURE
why we need to teach for tomorrow

David Hicks and Cathie Holden

tb
Trentham Books

VISIONS OF THE FUTURE

First published in 1995 by Trentham Books Limited

Trentham Books Limited
Westview House
734 London Road
Oakhill
Stoke-on-Trent
Staffordshire
England ST4 5NP

British Cataloguing in Publication Data
A catalogue record for this book is available from the British Library.

ISBN: 1 85856 030 6

Also by David Hicks

Minorities: A Teacher's Resource Book for the Multi-ethnic Curriculum (1981)

Teaching World Studies: An Introduction to Global Perspectives in the Curriculum
(1982) with Charles Townley

World Studies 8-13: A Teacher's Handbook (1985) with Simon Fisher

Education for Peace: Issues, Principles and Practice in the Classroom (1988)
Editor

Making Global Connections: A World Studies Workbook (1989)
Editor with Miriam Steiner

Educating for the Future: A Practical Classroom Guide (1994)

Preparing for the Future: Notes and Queries for Concerned Educators (1994)
Editor

Cover painting: Burning Landscape (detail) by Michael Thorogood

Designed and typeset by Trentham Print Design, Chester and
printed in Great Britain by Bemrose Shafron (Printers) Limited, Chester

To all futures educators:
yesterday, today and tomorrow

Contents

Tables

Figures

Preface

This book arises out the work of the Global Futures Project which was set up in 1989 to help teachers and students think more critically and creatively about the future. It is one of a series of publications highlighting the need for a more futures-orientated education for the twenty-first century. *Educating for the Future: A Practical Classroom Guide*, sets out the rationale for a futures dimension in the National Curriculum and provides a range of exemplar classroom activities. *Preparing for the Future: Notes and Queries for Concerned Educators*, brings together a selection of key readings on futures and futures education for those involved in initial and further teacher education.

Visions of the Future is the third book in this series. It highlights the crucial role that images of the future play in society and explores young people's current hopes and fears for the future. It arises out of collaborative research between David Hicks at Bath College of Higher Education and Cathie Holden at the University of Exeter. Our shared interest in children and the future has made this collaboration both fruitful and enjoyable.

The book weaves together several key themes. Part One focuses on the importance of a futures dimension in the curriculum. Chapter 1 looks at the crucial role of education in turbulent times and the need for educators to be more forward looking. Chapter 2 reminds teachers of the social importance of images of the future and of the value of work done by futurists and others. Chapter 3 reviews the research on adult and young people's views of the future over the last thirty years.

Part Two describes the findings of a research study carried out with nearly four hundred pupils aged 7 to 18. This focused on their hopes and fears for the future, personally, locally and globally. Chapters 4 and 5 describe the findings for primary and secondary age pupils respectively, whilst chapter 6 examines how findings varied with age and gender. Finally, Part Three contains examples of recent curriculum initiatives in Britain and Australia (chapter 7) and concludes (chapter 8) by stressing the need for new guiding images of a more sustainable twenty-first century.

This book would not have been possible without the expertise and support of many people. In particular we are most grateful for the co-operation of staff and students from participating schools in Avon, Devon, Somerset and Wiltshire. At the University of Exeter, Tricia Nash and Christabel Owens provided invaluable assistance with data handling whilst Martin Hughes and Edith Jayne kindly read drafts of the text. I would like to thank various educators for support, advice or comments on this book, in particular Karl Berger, Elise Boulding, Frank Hutchinson, Bernadette O'Rourke, Kathleen Rundall and Rick Slaughter. At Newton Park I constantly value the support of my colleagues Kay Wood and Andy Bord. My students on Global Futures and International Education and Change also support me in different ways. Other colleagues who inspire my work, although they would not all agree with the arguments here, are John Fien, John Huckle and Patrick Whitaker.

David Hicks
February 1995

PART ONE — REMEMBERING THE FUTURE

Chapter 1

Education for the Future

> By adding a future dimension to the learning process, we help to
> provide direction, purpose, and greater meaning to whatever is being
> studied. By integrating past, present, and future we act to strengthen
> a neglected link in the learning process. — Fitch and Svengalis

The last decade of a century seems an appropriate time for looking
backwards at what has passed and forwards to what might come. It is
certainly a time for educators to review both their own work and the
broader role of education within society. What should the role of education
be in these turbulent times as we approach the millennium — the same as
usual, something a little different, or something very different? We live
in a period characterised by loss of societal direction and purpose. What
should concerned educators be doing at such a time? Is the answer a
narrowly defined 'back to basics,' a prescribed National Curriculum, or
could it be something more exciting?

If one of the central roles of education is to prepare young people for
the future we need to ask why exploration of the future is a neglected issue
in education. The National Curriculum entitles pupils to preparation for
'the opportunities, responsibilities and experiences of adult life' and yet
offers little guidance on what education for a more sustainable society in
the twenty-first century might look like. In part these dilemmas, and this
loss of direction, arise because we lack guiding visions for the future.

3

Images of the future play a central role in social and cultural change at both personal and societal levels. It is important to know about people's hopes and fears for the future because they influence what individuals and groups are prepared to do, or not do, in the present. Images of the future in Western society are often pessimistic, envisaging a future worse than today. Such negative images can be indicators of a society in decline. Positive images of the future are important because they can help give a society direction and purpose.

This book explores what is known about people's views of the future and, in particular, what young people are thinking and feeling today. It arises out of work conducted by the authors which shows that primary and secondary pupils are concerned about a wide range of issues ranging from war, the environment and crime, to health, unemployment and personal relationships. It shows how these concerns change and develop between the ages of 7 and 18 and provides important information for teachers concerned with the humanities, citizenship, personal and social education, global and environmental education.

This book is ground-breaking in its scope and focus, for it brings together three hitherto neglected areas of teaching and research. These are:

- Why views of the future are important to society and how these have changed during the twentieth century.

- What children's interests are in personal, local and global issues today and their hopes and fears for the future.

- The need for a more explicit futures dimension in the curriculum at all levels of education.

Approaching the millennium

These times

One reason why interest in the future is growing is due to the approach of the third millennium. Whilst this may be dismissed as only a socio-temporal construct on the Christian calendar it nevertheless symbolises a potential turning point in human affairs. In 2001 CE a last decade turns into a first, one century changes into another, and we move from the second to the third millennium. Few people see such temporal changes in their lifetime.

The millennium provides a metaphor for change, encouraging questions about past and future directions for human society. It invites assessment of what has gone, what should be left behind and what taken forward, an inventory of the twentieth century. Whilst the 1890s saw an outburst of technological optimism for the coming new century the 1990s are very different. Developments in science and technology, whether military or economic, have not brought about the creation of the good society for all. Indeed globally they have only brought wealth and benefit to the few.

The millennium can thus act as a mirror for society, reflecting where we've come from and where we are now. It can also offer a doorway to where we want to go. But what are the images of the future that we project through that doorway into the twenty-first century? Is it to be the Golden Age or the Apocalypse, utopia or dystopia? The answer is probably neither but, as we approach the twenty-first century, interest in the future, both personal and societal, grows. There may be no facts about the future but it *is* that part of history which is still open to change.

Current global trends

There is no shortage of information about the current state of the planet and there is growing agreement about the seriousness of the global crisis we face. Each year the Worldwatch Institute in Washington publishes its *State of the World* report and Lester Brown recently set the scene (1993) with these words:

> In early 1992, the US National Academy of Sciences and the Royal Society of London issued a report that began: 'If current predictions of population growth prove accurate and patterns of human activity on the planet remain unchanged, science and technology may not be able to prevent either irreversible degradation of the environment or continued poverty for much of the world'... This abandonment of the technological optimism that has permeated so much of the twentieth century by two of the world's leading scientific bodies represents a major shift, but perhaps not a surprising one given the deteriorating state of the planet.

Brown goes on to point out that it is not just scientists that are concerned about such deterioration but people everywhere. In essence the two major global trends are that damage to the biosphere continues to increase, whilst

5

improvements to human welfare continue to decrease. Some commentators focus on the environment as the key problem, others on the human condition. The two are inextricably interrelated.

Stating the problem at a global scale clearly masks major local and national differences. During the eighties the gap between the rich and poor countries of the world continued to grow. By 1989 the richest fifth of the world's population had 80% of global trade and GNP. By contrast the poorest fifth of the world's population had less than 2%. The globalisation of consumer capitalism with its constant need for profit ensures that the countries of the periphery are actively underdeveloped by a process of unequal exchange. At the same time over-consumption, overindulgence and waste in the core countries of North America, Western Europe and Japan, are leading to a deep impoverishment of the spirit.

A psychology of denial

People respond to such mounting dilemmas in a variety of ways. Anthony Giddens argues that in trying to respond to such intractable problems as environmental disasters, civil war and abuse of human rights, we are faced with loss of meaning.

> Personal meaninglessness — the feeling that life has nothing worthwhile to offer — becomes a fundamental psychic problem in circumstances of late modernity. We should understand this phenomenon in terms of a repression of moral questions which day- to-day life poses, but which are denied answers. 'Existential isolation' is not so much a separation of individuals from others as a separation from the moral resources necessary to live a full and satisfying existence (Giddens, 1990).

It is not surprising that contemporary global issues are met by a variety of denials. 'Faced with this degree of change, we are tempted to deny the severity of environmental threats, and to assume we can get by with minor adjustments to business-as-usual. We elect politicians who validate our belief that the workings of the world are basically in order,' writes Sandra Postel (1992). The value of such denial is that it saves us from having to face the problems or thinking about what needs to be done.

Such psychological responses play a major role in both creating and sustaining the global crisis. By dimming awareness of unpleasant truths we create blind spots. Will Keepin (1991) explains:

> The means to dim awareness span the full range of classical defence mechanisms: denial, repression, sublimation, and so forth. The resulting blind spots are zones of self-deception, and they operate at every level from the individual to societal to national and international...A related psychological reality of the ecological crisis is widespread fear and despair among the general population about the future of the natural environment. Not dissimilar from the spectre of global nuclear war, there is a general sense of impending environmental doom, which causes depression, apathy, and environmental psychic numbing.

What should the role of education be in such times? Should it look back to the past and attempt to find secure ground in what has gone before or should it accept the challenge of change and look forward to the future?

Transformative education

Attention has already been drawn to the entitlement that pupils have under the National Curriculum to preparation for the responsibilities, opportunities and experiences of adult life. Those starting primary school now will be adults by the second decade of the new century and their adulthood will last well into the latter part of the century. Teachers therefore have a legal responsibility to prepare pupils for life in the period 1995- 2070.

This casts new light on the meaning of 'education for the future.' Rather than being narrowly defined as careers or personal and social education, education for the future requires a much deeper and broader response. This is perhaps why it is a term little used by traditionalist educators. Before elaborating on this, however, it is important to clarify the view of education that underlies such a concern.

The role of education

In his work on environmental education John Fien (1993a) highlights differing ideological orientations to the world and also to education. Such ideologies differ in how they perceive the purpose of education, the social role of the school, the curriculum, and teaching and learning itself. Whilst

Table 1.1 — Ideological orientations

Conservative
Schools prepare students for work; maintain and legitimise exist-ing social, economic and political structures; formal classrooms and subject teaching; directive transmission of knowledge; pur-pose: to learn your place.

Reformative
School prepares students to participate in the reform of society; more informal and individualised classroom; less rigid subject framework; person-centred facilitation of learning; purpose: to learn who you are

Transformative
School and society reflect one another; mixed ability group work; flexible boundaries between school and community; teacher as a resource person; school has role to play in challenging social, political and economic inequalities; purpose: to transform self and society.

Table 1. 2 — Studying an issue

1. What is the issue?
What do we think, feel, hope and fear, in relation to this particular issue? What do others who are involved think, feel and say?

2. How has it come about?
Why do we and others think, feel and act the way we do? What and who has influenced us and others involved? What is the history of this situation?

3. Who gains, who loses?
Who has the power in this situation and how do they use it? Is it used to the advantage of some and the disadvantage of others? If so, in what way?

4. What is our vision?
What would things look like in a more just, peaceful and sustainable future, for ourselves and for others? What values will we use to guide our choices?

5. What can be done?
What are the possible courses of action open to us? What are others already doing? Which course of action is most likely to achieve our vision of a preferred future?

6. How will we do it?
How shall we implement our plan of action in school, at home, or in the community? How shall we work together? Whose help might we need? How do we measure our success?

the summary in Table 1.1 is an over-simplification of educational practice it nevertheless highlights key values differences amongst educators.

In the light of such differing assumptions environmental educators have drawn an important distinction between education *about* the environment and education *for* the environment. Teaching *about* the environment would thus be part of the conservative/reformative tradition. There is information that the student needs to have about environmental matters in order to become a responsible member of society. Teaching for the environment, however, goes further in recognising that the issues require both critical reflection and action in everyday life.

The same holds true, we believe, in relation to futures. Thus teaching *about* the future does nothing to prepare students actively for a tomorrow that will be very different from today. It merely tells them what might happen. Education *for* the future, on the other hand, requires exploration of their own and others' hopes and fears for the future and the action required to create a more just and ecologically sustainable future. It empowers children to feel that they can work towards their chosen future. This book is written from just such a transformative perspective.

It begins in the classroom with the study of issues that are relevant to the pupils themselves: litter in the playground, experiments on animals, racist abuse, maybe, or dangerous traffic. All such issues have local and global components and the interrelationships between the two soon emerge. Education *for* the future also requires that questions such as those shown in Table 1.2 be asked over any issue (Hicks, 1994a).

Questions such as these lie at the heart of good education in a democratic society. If children are to grow up to become empowered and responsible citizens it will be because they have learnt and practised these skills in school.

New movements in education

Before looking at what education for the future might imply in practice it is important to locate such a concern in its historical context. Ian Lister, in writing about the development of political education (1987), highlights the key role of what he calls the new movements in education. He is referring here to a diverse range of educational initiatives during the 80s, ranging from world studies/global education, peace education and development education, to human rights education, multicultural education and environmental education.

Lister comments:

> The twin stresses on human-centred education and global perspectives constitute a radical shift away from the dominant tradition of schooling (which is knowledge centred and ethnocentric). Thus the vanguard educators seek to give to education a new *process* and a new *perspective* on the world. The new movements have eight important features, all of which distinguish them from conventional social education...

These shared beliefs, Lister suggests, are that i) knowledge should aim at improving the human condition; ii) the curriculum should include major issues such as war and peace, poverty and development; iii) learning should also be about the acquisition of skills; iv) skill development requires active learning; v) education should be affective as well as cognitive; vi) pluralism and diversity need to be recognised and valued; vii) there should be a global perspective in the curriculum; viii) education should also have a futures perspective.

Much of the most innovative work in education over the last fifteen years has come from those promoting the need for global education and development education. A range of materials, conferences and in-service training programmes during the eighties put the UK in the forefront of such developments. These came from organisations such as the Centre for Global Education, the World Studies 8-13 project, the National Association of Development Education Centres and the World Studies Network. A good flavour of these initiatives can be gained from Robin Richardson (1990) and David Hicks (1990). A concern for the future was often present in this work and best exemplified in resources such as *Global Teacher, Global Learner* (Pike and Selby, 1988) and *World Studies 8-13: A Teacher's Handbook* (Fisher and Hicks, 1985).

Education for the future can thus be seen as a concern rooted in the new movements and in the entitlement offered by the National Curriculum. Whilst the latter only refers to the future in an implicit way, global education can provide experience of exploring the future in a more explicit way. By putting these two together it is possible to map out what a critical education for the future might look like.

Children's images of the future

The experienced teacher always takes into account what her pupils bring to a new learning situation, be it knowledge of distant places or their understanding of science. Children are not blank tablets, nor does schooling take place in a cultural vacuum. In the same way that children have preconceptions and stereotypes about other countries, so they also make a range of assumptions about the future. In large part these come from portrayals of the future in popular films, advertisements, television, books, comics, computer games and toys.

Children's images of the future are thus likely to be stereotyped and critically unreflective. One of the few people to investigate contemporary images of the future in children's media is Frank Hutchinson (1994). He particularly makes a distinction between explicit and implicit images of the future and argues that the latter are by far the most common. Also that implicit images by definition rule out any discussion of alternative futures. In looking at children's toys, Hutchinson reports:

> Important connections probably exist between the selective processes of childhood political socialisation, on the one hand, and restricted consciousness about alternatives to sexist, militarist and technocratic futures on the other. If there are strongly selective traditions that condone or legitimate certain behaviour as 'normal' or 'inevitable' and marginalise others, then taken-for-granted assumptions about the future are likely to be powerfully propagated.

Thus a steady diet of toys and games which offer aggressive male role-models, often with the use of hi-tech fire power, contains within it implicit views of how life in the future will be. Such toys are not conducive to creative play, co-operative learning or development of the social imagination. Toys are often promoted in relation to films and TV programmes to meet, in the words of the merchandisers, 'market demand.' However, the power to define interest and need actually lies with the merchandiser and film maker. An interesting parallel exists with toys targeted at girls, with their unchallenging notions of beauty, passivity and homecare (Dixon, 1990).

In looking at widely used school textbooks in Australia, Hutchinson notes that little attention is paid to critical or alternative perspectives on issues, particularly in science and economic texts. For example, whilst half of all scientific research and development is devoted to military-related projects this is seldom stated in school textbooks. Indeed scientific and economic texts give non-existent or only very brief treatment to the problem of war. Whilst nearly 60% of history, geography and other social science books give extensive treatment to war, less than a fifth offer any non-violent alternatives to resolving conflicts. War thus appears as a fact of life, not something that can be queried, debated, or contested. There is no notion of less-violent alternative futures.

Like interactive computer games comics are pitched mostly at the adolescent male. Amongst the most popular sellers are those such as *2000 AD* and *Judge Dredd*. Hutchinson (1994) summarises:

> In all these titles there is a strong tendency to foreclosure of the future. There are recurring ideological themes of militarism, sexism and technocratism. It is overwhelmingly a threat-filled and crisis-ridden mindscape of the future but one in which present feelings of aliena-tion, powerlessness and relentless change may be compensated for through 'hi-tech' answers and Nietzschean, superhero violence.

Many computer games also show a similar poverty of the imagination. Future worlds are tunnel-visioned and the cultural message, rather than being one of democratic participation and action, is a 'flight of escapism or the fight of macho violence and machine-dependency in an insecure, fragmenting and crisis-filled mindscape of what might be.'

One might expect TV programmes, especially those used in school, to offer a more critical view of the future. However, the common view of the future, Hutchinson reports, is also one of foreclosure on social alternatives. Developments in science and technology are often treated in a 'techno-wizardry' fashion as a sign of inexorable progress, rather than analysed critically for their social and environmental impact and as issues for ethical debate.

Toys, games, textbooks, comics and TV, therefore often give a circum-scribed view of the future. This is often a gender-stereotyped future and one in which science and technology are seen to provide all the answers. People are not shown as active agents of their destiny but rather as reacting to the inevitability of 'human nature' or 'technological progress.' In either case the future is shown as something not to be actively created but rather passively anticipated. The future has been colonised well before we reach it. So the task for teachers is crucial and critical. Such images need to be made the subject of critical investigation and research. As later chapters will show, such imagery becomes self-defeating unless challenged. Students need to be given the opportunity to generate imagery of alternative futures which explore more peaceful, just and sustainable themes.

Learning for change

A futures dimension

Time and space are the two major axes of human existence and it is their exploration which underlies much of the curriculum. On the spatial dimension education helps children to make sense of their world, from the personal and local to the national and global. On the temporal dimension education explores the past and the present, but often pays less attention to the future. It is anticipation of the future, however, which motivates behaviour in the present. Most difficult decisions require making a choice between alternative futures.

If I've experienced some control over my life in the past then the future may appear a place of promise.Whereas, if my experience was of having had no control over events, then the future may be a place to fear. Images of the future thus play a crucial role in relation to our behaviour and actions in the present. This is true at both personal and societal levels.

Noel Gough (1988a) examined a range of educational documents to see how they conceptualised the future. 'Even a cursory analysis of educational discourse reveals its temporal assymetry. That is, by comparison to the future, the temporal categories of past and present receive more frequent and more explicit attention,' he writes. All educational writers, he argues, implicitly use some concept of the future and these can often be discerned even when not overtly described. They tend to be tacit inferences, token invocations or taken-for-granted assumptions.

'Tacit futures' are those which are implied but never clearly stated. The National Curriculum entitlement to preparation for adult life is one example. Thus the word 'future' rarely occurs in such documents and is certainly not defined in any way, but is implicitly there. Tacit futures are virtually invisible except to the practised eye.

'Token futures' are a little more visible. They involve some reference to futures concepts, but only in a rhetorical fashion. They lack substance or explanation, as in references to 'education for the future' or 'education

14

for the twenty-first century'. What at first appears to be explicitly about the future turns out to be a token reference. As Gough says 'When one finds 'the future' (or a futures-oriented reference) in the title of an educational document it usually means much less than might be expected'.

'Taken-for-granted futures' are the most visible of the three. A particular view of the future is proposed, but its virtues or likelihood are not questioned in any way. It is not offered as one amongst several alternative possible futures. The most common taken-for-granted futures are those which assume that increased economic growth will resolve all problems or that all developments in science and technology represent 'progress.'

To correct the temporal imbalance found in educational discourse, the taught curriculum, and in teaching materials, we need to move beyond these limited perspectives. The futures dimension in the curriculum involves appreciation of the fact that we have a choice of alternative futures before us. It involves the exploration of what those different futures, personal and global, might be. It requires that we examine the values and assumptions behind different views of the future. It means careful exploration of probable futures (those that seem most *likely* to come about) and of preferable futures (those that we feel *ought* to come about). It requires that we help students to develop skills of foresight for the times ahead. It is a concern which needs to be more explicit in all subject areas of the curriculum.

Teaching for tomorrow

What might a socially critical education for the future look like and what would it involve? Many of the key issues were set out in Alvin Toffler's *Learning For Tomorrow* (1974) and subsequently developed in curricula terms by American educators. In the UK it was the new movements in education, and particularly global education, which brought this concern into the curriculum. A variety of exemplar activities can be found in the work of the World Studies 8-13 project (Fisher and Hicks, 1985), the Centre for Global Education (Pike and Selby, 1988) and the Global Futures Project (Hicks, 1993a). Recent examples of American classroom materials can be found in Haas (1988), Riley (1989) and Whaley (1991).

Some flavour of the breadth of concern can also be gained from titles of classroom activities: My Future, Making Forecasts, Mental Maps,

Projects For a Better World, A New Society, Action for Change, Imaging the Future, Trend Extrapolation, Futures Wheel, Delphi Technique, Values and the Future. Experience shows that pupils find such issues to be of great interest. The future matters to them in a different way than it does to adults, who have less of the future before them to anticipate.

In the UK the National Curriculum provides the main framework for planning teaching and learning. During the eighties many teachers incorporated global and futures themes into their work because they felt them to be important and of value to the pupils. However, the initial content overload of the National Curriculum, the increase in teacher assessment, and the delegation of funding to schools, led to a narrowing of focus on specific subject demands.

Since the future was only a tacit concern, the temporal imbalance in the curriculum remained. The slimming down of the National Curriculum from 1995, however, means more time available for cross-curricular concerns such as environmental education and citizenship which, by definition, require a futures perspective. What that perspective looks like in different subject areas has been spelt out by Hicks (1994) in *Education for the Future: A Practical Classroom Guide*. It now needs subject specialists to elaborate further on the contribution that their subject can make to the futures dimension in the curriculum.

But education for the future is more than a collection of classroom activities, however innovative and effective they may be. In particular it requires a slow process of legitimation which sets out for teachers and others the broader educational context of these matters. Quite clearly, a good deal goes on in the futures field which could be of use to teachers (Slaughter, 1993). However, at present, this is to be found in specialist journals such as *Futures* and *Futures Research Quarterly*. Those with an interest in futures and education now have an important role to play in legitimating futures education in schools.

For example, Frank Hutchinson, who worked as a teacher, curriculum developer and textbook writer in the fields of global education and peace education, drew these interests together in his doctoral thesis, *Futures Consciousness and the School* (1992). It is one of the best studies available of the need for futures education. Hedley Beare and Richard Slaughter (1993), in their *Education for the Twenty-First Century*, have written a thoughtful and challenging text for all educators. It sets a concern for the future in its broader socio-cultural context, that is, the nature of industrialism and its consequences, the growing development of a global consciousness and the need to move beyond scientific materialism. Allyson Holbrook, in an article entitled 'Teachers with vision and visions of teaching,' (1992) has also described the way in which she uses futures studies in her postgraduate work with teachers.

A sustainable society

The Earth Summit in 1992 focused the world's attention on the relationship between environmental and development issues and the need for a more sustainable form of development in the future. The term itself is a contested one. It is used to mean anything from 'accelerated economic growth in order to raise living standards and protect the environment' to the 'integration of social, ecological and economic goals on an equal basis in a low or no-growth society.' Certainly *the* issue of the twenty-first century must be whether we can create a more just and ecologically sustainable society for ourselves and future generations.

This provides a clear focus for work in futures education. Not only do we need to explore the origins, nature and consequences of current unsustainable practices but we need also to establish the need for, and nature of, a more sustainable society at both local and global levels. This is the task for the future and one which educators are now beginning to address. Books such as David Orr's *Ecological Literacy: Education and the Transition to a Postmodern World* (1992) and Gregory Smith's *Education and the Environment: Learning to Live with Limits* (1992) mark out the deep cultural territory that has to be explored and the profound choices that have to be made.

Summary

This opening chapter has set the scene for a study of images of the future by highlighting three concerns. Firstly, that the approaching millennium will prompt greater interest in the future and reflection on what society wishes to leave behind and what to take forward into the new century — in particular current global trends, as discussed at the Earth Summit in 1992, and their likely impact on the future. The magnitude of such issues can sometimes lead to a psychology of denial wherein people minimise or even ignore the threats facing the planet.

Next, education has an important role to play in times of turbulent change. For education to prepare young people for the changes ahead, it needs to take a transformative orientation that promotes the skills needed for critical reflection and action. The new movements in education have a crucial role to play in developing a futures perspective and counteracting the negative images of the future promoted by popular culture. The various influences on children's images of the future are generally uni-dimensional and gender-stereotyped.

Finally, educating more explicitly for the future is vital, yet current study of the future is marginalised in educational discourse and curriculum practice. Sources of useful materials for teachers and teacher educators exist, and the crucial role schools play in helping to create a more sustainable society cannot be over-emphasised.

Chapter 2

Understanding the Future

> Futures studies is not study of the future — as nobody can know what
> the future will be like... We do not believe that it is possible to predict
> the future. What futures studies mainly does is to study ideas people
> have now about the future, what I call their images of the future. It
> tries to find out how these images influence the way people act now,
> and how people's present actions influence the future. — Jim Dator

If the future needs to be made a more central concern in education, then
educators need to become more aware of the work carried out by futurists.
This chapter begins by sketching out the diversity of concerns found in
the 'futures field' and, in particular, the importance of futures studies. It
then goes on to consider the crucial role that images of the future play in
social and cultural change and the way in which such images have
changed during the the twentieth century. Finally, attention is drawn to
the ideological differences that underlie all conceptualisations of the
future.

Futures and futurists

A growing interest
Concern for the future is an inescapable, indeed essential, element of the
human condition. The future matters because it is where we will spend
the rest of our lives. It is that part of history which is still open to change,

that part of time still potentially open to some measure of control. Whilst people's prime concern is generally with their personal futures, these are inextricably bound up with broader societal and global futures. Interest in the wider future has grown rapidly during the course of the twentieth century, due in part to the growing impact of social, technological and environmental change.

Such change has been prompted largely by the constant demands of consumer capitalism and the military-industrial complex. As the pace of change has quickened, many individuals, groups and organisations have come to realise that the future requires much more careful consideration. In the past, when change was slower, the future was likely to be very similar to the present. In a sense it therefore required less attention. Today however, the future often seems to arrive too quickly and unpredictably.

All human choices, all acts of production and consumption, have future consequences for the individual, the environment and other people, yet we often choose to act as if this were not the case. Many of the consequences of technological innovation, for example, turn out to be both unforeseen and harmful, be it pesticides in the water supply, cities choked with traffic, or the deaths caused by Chernobyl. Learning only from hindsight is a costly way of moving forwards. Both the scope and pace of change now require that we develop greater skills of foresight (Slaughter, 1995).

The range of issues affecting the future health of society is wide, from factory farming and depletion of the ozone layer, to increasing crime rates and violent conflict. One important guide to the problems most urgently requiring attention is the diversity of new social movements that have emerged since the 1960s in response to such issues. Their focus ranges from civil rights, peace and gender equality, to ecology, race and land rights (Scott, 1992). Such social movements play an important historical role in shaping the intellectual and cultural climate. They warn of dangers ahead and they stimulate radical questioning of the status quo. They provide glimpses of preferable futures and offer potential guidelines towards their realisation.

There are, of course, many reasons why people choose *not* to take an interest in the future. For most people on the planet day-to-day survival is the main priority and the future may thus be measured only in days or hours. If people have little control over their lives or fear for the future, then a live-for-today philosophy makes most sense. Yet even under the harshest conditions people may still work for the better future they believe in, as shown by the ending of apartheid in South Africa.

Interest is also growing in the notion of the rights of future generations. Economists, philosophers, international lawyers and others have begun to raise questions about what our obligations should be to unborn generations. (Weiss, 1989) This is a significant step forward in futures consciousness, for it asks us to imagine the rights that future generations, our children, grandchildren and great-grandchildren might wish to have. That their ancestors should have considered their welfare might well be the deepest wish of future generations.

The futures field

Futures research emerged in the post-war period, with other multi-disciplinary concerns such as peace research, to deal with the challenges of a new world scene. In particular the demands of the military-industrial complex and the growing rate of technological change made future-orientated research a high priority. A major reason for its development was its value to business planners, economic thinkers, technology forecasters, social and policy scientists. Over the years a broader futures field has emerged which encompasses a spectrum of concerns.

Hedley Beare and Richard Slaughter (1993) suggest that the field has three main foci: futures research, futures studies and futures movements. Futures research lies at the 'hard' pole of this spectrum, with a knowledge-seeking emphasis on prediction, economic and technical forecasting, systems analysis and management science. The main emphasis is on specialist forecasting and planning, through the use of analytic and quantitative methods. Such research is generally for government departments and large organisations, so little known to the public.

Futures movements, with their emphasis on radical social change, are at the 'soft' pole of the spectrum, and embrace speculative writing, social networking, new social movements and alternative lifestyles. The women's movement, the peace movement and the environmental movement would be cases in point. Although few people involved with these concerns would consider themselves futurists per se, most are impelled by their visions of more desirable social futures.

Between these two poles futures studies attempts to synthesise and communicate many of these concerns through scenario writing, comparative surveys and critiques of futures issues, and the study of futures in education. It encompasses academics, critics, writers and educators who may be involved in specialist work but who wish also to communicate futures ideas to a wider audience.

Michael Marien, however (1985), argues that there is no such thing as a futures field because practitioners have far too disparate a range of interests and do not share a common academic background. Futures cannot therefore be nominated as a proper field of enquiry. The fact remains that the future has increasingly become a focus of concern amongst specialists and generalists alike, as witnessed by the literature reviewed in Marien's (1994) *Future Survey Annual,* published each year by the World Future Society. In this he attempts to 'consider both hopes and fears, to bridge global and national perspectives, to identify and combine multiple perspectives, and to reconcile realists and idealists.'

Futures debates

Sohail Inayatullah (1993) suggests that 'futures studies largely straddles two dominant modes of knowledge — the technical, concerned with predicting the future and the humanist, concerned with developing a good society.' The former often involves extrapolation from current trends in an attempt to predict and control the future. The focus of concern is on probable futures. The latter, conversely, is values driven and focuses on identifying preferable futures which embody the good society. Jim Dator, (1994) in the quotation that opens this chapter, highlights the importance of the second category and the way in which individuals, organisations and cultures create categories for viewing the future.

There was considerable debate about alternative futures in the 1970s, largely prompted by the publication of *The Limits to Growth* (Meadows *et al*, 1972). One of the first major attempts at global computer modelling, this study argued that, as a result of population growth, pollution, consumption and depletion of resources, global collapse was unavoidable in the twenty-first century. It lead to a lengthy debate about the possible limits to growth which in part polarised around optimistic/pessimistic premises about the future itself (Freeman and Jahoda, 1978).

In 1985 Barry Hughes reassessed the futures debate and offered an analysis of the world views proposed in different studies, noting that:

> Images of the future remain as diverse as they were a decade ago. Clearly, either basic data needed to understand where we are and where we are going are simply unavailable or analysts are talking past each other, proceeding on different assumptions and understanding and selecting the data according to different criteria.

The eighties, however, saw few major studies of the future. Peter Moll (1991) suggests that the current futures field is more scattered and difficult to grasp because long-term research and futures studies are less politically acceptable in times of neo-conservatism and market-orientated economic policies, .

Both Moll (1991) and Marien (1992) have suggested that the new rallying point for futurists in the 1990s may well be the debate about the need for an ecologically sustainable future. Marien notes that the widespread concern over environmental issues and the increasing use of 'sustainable' and 'green' to denote desirable futures suggests a new futures movement. Clearly, as we approach the end of the century, the global problematique will prompt increased debate about the future. The publication of *Beyond the Limits*, (Meadows, 1993) for example, reopens the debate about global collapse and sustainable futures.

Images of the future

Importance of images

The ability to hold images of other events, places and times whether real or imaginary, in the mind's eye, is a distinguishing features of our species. It allows us to be present at events in time past, to recall places we have visited and others we have not. We can also create images of imaginary places and imaginary pasts. It enables us to look at situations, problems and obstacles, and ponder alternative and better ways of resolving them.

Representing the future through use of the creative imagination is a natural and necessary human activity. Future events and situations are thus anticipated through the imagination. What is likely to happen if this course of action is chosen? What are the likely consequences of setting this train of events in motion? Wendell Bell and James Mau (1971) proposed the following definition of images of the future:

23

An image of the future is an expectation about the state of things to come at some future time. We may think most usefully of such expectations as a range of differentially probable possibilities rather than as a single point on a continuum.

Active imaging can be used to consider what will probably happen in the future and also what we would like to happen. It may be in the near or distant future and may relate to personal, societal or global concerns.

The images that we hold of the future motivate and influence what we choose to do in the present. If we anticipate failure we may choose *not* to undertake a particular activity. If we fear the future, as many young people did during the nuclear arms race, then a live-for-today philosophy may be the result. Having faith in our abilities may persuade us to reach for greater heights in the future. If life today is not to our satisfaction, for ourselves or others, we may strive to create a better and fairer world in the future.

Images of the future are constantly being negotiated by different interest groups in society: politicians, business, religious groups or the media. We are surrounded by competing images of the future and it is the groups with most power in society which generally offer the most compelling images. Indeed some images may be so strong that no other views of the future are imaginable. In western society the pervading images of the future are those promoted by white, middle class males, since they generally occupy the positions of power in most sectors of society. The future, or rather the imagination, can thus be colonised so that we fail to see how things could be different.

There are many ways of categorising images of the future. For example, images can be categorised by geographical scale, i.e. local, national, global, or by temporal scale, i.e. short, middle and long-term futures. Alternatively one can have images of the worst, best and most likely futures or of possible, probable and preferable futures. Possible futures are all those which could conceivably come about, probable futures are those which we expect to come about and preferable futures are all those we feel should come about.

Pessimistic or worst case images of the future abound in the media and literature of western society. They are often apocalyptic in nature and may, for example, deal with the situation of post-holocaust survivors, whether in the aftermath of nuclear war, eco-catastrophe or breakdown of law and order. They are amongst the most common images of the future in films,

TV and science fiction novels. They are also part of a wider anti-utopian or dystopian tradition in speculative writing. Pessimistic images of the future can result in psychic numbing and inaction or, alternatively, their very negativity can lead to vigorous action to avert them.

Most people are locked into images of their probable, i.e. expected future, whether personal or societal. On the one hand this is necessary since most of our energy needs to be devoted to what is likely to happen. But it can also be limiting if it results in unquestioning attitudes to the status quo. Images of the probable future can lead to people making the best of things or just getting on with life. Sometimes images of the probable future may coincide with pessimistic or worst case scenarios.

Preferable futures are all those which people feel *should* come about in order to realise the values that they most cherish. The growing interest in the nature of more just and ecologically sustainable futures is one example. Thus a study of images of the future is important because they can provide the incentive for cultures or societies to advance. Images of preferable futures are crucial because they provide both hope and the motivation to change things. They also relate to a long utopian tradition in western society, both literary and lived, which stresses the need to explore the nature of the good life and the good society (Kumar, 1991).

A mirror of the times

The first writer to deal explicitly and in depth with images of the future was the Dutch social scientist Fred Polak (1972). In his detailed study of the historical role of such images in western society he chronicles how, from Sumerian times onwards, the creative imagining of the 'totally other' has acted as a powerful magnet drawing a society on towards its envisioned future. Images of the future, he argues, act as 'guiding stars for human civilisation.'

Elise Boulding (1978), who learnt Dutch in order to translate Polak's work into English, describes this broad sweep thus:

> The great futuristic visions of medieval Christian Europe, further powered by the voyages of discovery and the birth of the 15th and 16th centuries, are now history. We can find in the utopias of the succeeding centuries the outlines of most of the infrastructure of modern society: in economics, the trade union movement, profit-sharing, social security, and scientific management; in the political order,

parliamentary democracy and universal suffrage; and in the social realm, universal education, welfare services, and 'emancipation' of women, the designing of New Towns, and the technology of social planning.

Polak argued that a society's images of the future act as a mirror of the times and reflect its inward essence. The history of a culture, he maintained, is reflected in the history of its images of the future. As images change and are worked through, fundamental changes in thinking and human awareness can occur. The future of a society can be measured by the power of its thinking about the future. Most crucially, he argues that the rise and fall of images of the future precedes the rise and fall of cultures. As long as a society's images of the future are positive and flourishing the culture blossoms, but once images begin to decay and lose their vitality the culture cannot long survive.

This argument lies at the heart of Polak's work and his warning to the world in the 1950s, when his book was first published, focused on what he saw as a dangerous decline in imaging capacity in western countries. As a society begins to disintegrate so do its images of the future and a negative feedback loop is set up. Polak saw the mid-twentieth century as being historically unique in only possessing negative images of the future. His timely contribution was thus to posit a vital relationship between the social imagination and social transformation.

Polak, of course, wrote before the burgeoning of interest in global issues during the sixties. Forty years on, there is still a dearth of imaging capacity. Moves have been made to rectify this, however. Boulding (1988) has developed Polak's work in consciously harnessing futures imaging to promote desirable social change. Originally a response to the nuclear arms race and the problem of imagining a world without weapons, she has worked with Robert Ziegler (1989) to create a repertoire of workshop techniques for envisioning more positive futures.

It *is* now perhaps possible to glimpse the emergence of new and positive guiding images of the future. Specifically these centre around notions of more just and ecologically sustainable futures. As already noted, Marien (1992) suggests that sustainability will provide a new focus for futures studies. What is still lacking in much of the current work on sustainability, however, are precisely the sorts of insights that futurists are able to offer (Hicks and Holden, 1995).

The twentieth century

The history of the last hundred years provides a salutary reminder of how images of the future may change. The last decade of the nineteenth century, for example, was a period of uncertainty but also of optimism. In 1897, on the occasion of Queen Victoria's Diamond Jubilee, the British Empire was at the height of its power. The progressive ideas of the period were encapsulated in a mood of optimism. Nature, it seemed, had finally been conquered and technological progress promised untold benefits and even greater achievements in the new century.

As the new century opened, H.G. Wells was composing his first survey of the future whilst Lenin, in Switzerland, was writing about what life would be like after the revolution. The Great War, however, totally shattered this sense of the beneficence of progress and images of the future were never to be the same again.

Clarke, (1992) chronicler of futures ideas and futures thinking, argues that:

> By the beginning of the 20th century, then, the idea of the future had been written into the agendas of the new age. The dominant mood of these early forecasts was a confident expectation of constant technological progress and steady social improvement. Their baseline rested on certain adamantine convictions — that Western society could only change for the better, that the applied sciences would always work to human advantage, and that the great European empires would continue for ever and ever.
>
> World War 1, however, changed these assumptions in most brutal ways; for one of the more painful lessons from that dreadful conflict was the revelation of an unforeseen void between expectations and subsequent events. After 1918 — in all but the most doggedly optimistic forecasts — a new uncertainty factor replaced the old certainties of universal progress. In Europe, where ancient monarchies had vanished and new nations had appeared, there were many doubts about the future of Western society.

The horrors of the war, the futility of trench warfare, the use of poison gas, the growth of aerial warfare, the development of the tank, all revealed the dark side of technological progress. It is a salutary fact that war is one of the most powerful promoters of futures thinking. New weapons, be it machine gun or Cruise missile, can for a time command the future.

As a result of the shocking impact of military technology on human life, the 1920s saw the beginning of a profound questioning about the relationship between technology, society and progress. It was clear that technological progress plus social organisation did not necessarily guarantee a better future after all. The mood of optimism about the future, so strong in the two decades before the war, rapidly evaporated, to be replaced by a sense of doubt and pessimism. The future now looked profoundly different.

This change in mood was also apparent in the life and writings of H.G. Wells. At the beginning of the century he dominated the new trend in futures thinking. He gave an authoritative address to the Royal Institution in 1902 on 'The discovery of the future'. He had high hopes for the future of humanity as reflected in his numerous books and articles on the future. By the end of his life, however, he too echoed the pessimism and disillusionment of his age.

In the 1930s, with the Great Depression and the spectre of war in Europe looming again, the future remained a place of fear rather than hope. When war came it was even more brutal and widespread than before, global in scope and with science and technology being used to develop the gas chambers of the Third Reich and the atomic bomb. Could the future look any worse than this?

With the advent of the nuclear arms race between the United States and the Soviet Union from 1945 to 1989, apocalyptic imagery of death and destruction came into its own. The future became a place of not just pessimism but deep despair and even greater fear. A spate of novels, films and TV programmes during this forty year period offered increasingly macabre images of human destiny. For a generation Orwell's 1984 offered a harsh and unrelenting portrayal of an authoritarian tomorrow. The long American war in Vietnam kept images of violence and destruction on our TV screens.

In the 1970s eco-catastrophe was added to the growing repertoire of Western dystopias. Any description of a utopian society was now set in the distant rather than the near future. The 1980s saw an acceleration of the arms race and a growing fear of nuclear war followed by nuclear winter. The 1990s, however, offer a period of reassessment. Whilst the dystopia of global war has receded, that of unsustainable economic growth and consequent environmental damage has not. In some ways they seem less paralysing than images of nuclear war. It is now time perhaps, to return not to the naive optimism of a century ago, but to come to a more qualified optimism about the future.

Differing perspectives

Images of the future, it should be clear, vary enormously depending on people's attitudes, values, priorities, hopes and fears. As Warren Wagar (1992) comments, 'The future is a very murky place. There are no eye-witness accounts, no first hand evidence. Worse still... all images of the future... are also shaped by the normative preconceptions of the enquirer.' The following examples illustrate some of the ways in which politics, culture, class and gender affect views of the future.

Future scenarios

At its simplest, the purpose of creating a scenario is to 'tell a story about the future'. It is a way of answering the question 'What if... ?' and provides an outline sketch of the major features of an alternative future. It is thus possible to explore how differing elements of a scenario might interact, what steps would be needed to achieve it, and its possible future conse-quences. Scenarios can be sketched with broad brush strokes or drawn more precisely, to provide a detailed framework for planning. In any situation a spread of scenarios is generally created in order to clarify the range of options available.

Creating future scenarios is not a neutral activity. Various ideological assumptions underlie all descriptions of the future, whether probable or preferable. Christopher Freeman and Marie Jahoda (1978), for example, drew on economic and political theory to identify three broad world-views: conservative, reformist and radical. Each of these world-views, they point out, makes very different prescriptions for the future. The conservative world-view prioritises individual self-interest, liberty and a free market economy. Reformists stress the need for greater democracy and equality and a substantial degree of state intervention to achieve this. Radicals believe in public ownership and democratic control of the means of production leading to social and political transformation of capitalist society.

A more recent use of scenarios is found in *The Geography of Europe's Futures* (Masser et al. 1992). As a result of analysing current trends and possibilities, scenarios are drawn for Europe in 2020 which focus on issues such as population, the economy, transport and communications. Three different scenarios are given for each issue, to highlight respectively: growth, equity, the environment. The growth scenarios highlight the likely outcome of policies that prioritise high-tech economic growth with little state intervention. The equity scenarios show what the impact would be of policies that prioritise the reduction of social and spatial inequalities. The environment scenarios show what is likely to happen if quality of life and environmental impact are the foremost concerns.

Slaughter (1993) uses five scenarios in his teaching: Breakdown; Repressive; Business-as-usual; Ecological Decentralist; and Transformational. A similar, but simplified, spectrum has been developed by Hicks (1994a) for use in the classroom. He provides double-page spreads of four differing scenarios for pupils to explore: More of the Same; Technological Fix; Edge of Disaster; and Sustainable Development. Pupils are encouraged to examine each scenario and decide whether people would like living in that future, what the good and difficult things are about it, and who in it is likely to benefit and who lose.

Yet in many scenarios crucial perspectives on the future have been omitted, since they have often been written from the perspective of white males in the northern hemisphere. They fail to portray the overriding concerns of Third World peoples or of women, i.e. two thirds and half of the human population respectively.

Cultural imperialism

An alternative discourse brings quite different perspectives and priorities. For example here is Eduardo Galeano, (1991) the Uruguayan writer:

There is just one place where yesterday and today meet, recognise each other and embrace, and that place is tomorrow. Certain voices from the American past, long past, sound very futuristic. For example, the ancient voice that still tells us we are children of the earth... (and) that speaks to us of community heralds another world as well. Community — the communal mode of production and life — is the oldest of American traditions... It belongs to the earliest days and the first people, but it also belongs to the times ahead and anticipates a

New World. For there is nothing less alien to these lands of ours than socialism. Capitalism, on the other hand, is foreign: like smallpox, like the flu. It came from abroad.

Or note Vandana Shiva, (1989) physicist and philosopher, on women, ecology and development:

> Seen from the experience of Third World women, the modes of thinking and action that pass for science and development, respectively, are not universal and humanly inclusive, as they are made out to be; modern science and development are projects of male, western origin, both historically and ideologically... The industrial revolution converted economics from the prudent management of resources for sustenance and basic needs satisfaction into a process of commodity production for profit maximisation... The new relationship of man's domination and mastery over nature was thus also associated with new patterns of domination and mastery over women, and their exclusion from participation as partners in both science and development.

It is easy in the West to see past, present, and future from an unexamined, indeed often unconscious, imperialist perspective. Scholars such as Noam Chomsky, in his *Year 501: The Conquest Continues*, (1993) and Edward Said in *Culture and Imperialism*, (1993) have shown in graphic detail how the genocide of colonial times and the exploitation of modern-day imperialism are related. The same issues have been raised in relation to future studies by writers such as Ziauddin Sardar (1993) who argues that the Western intellectual's preoccupation with post-modernism, far from being a global concern, is merely one more attempt to colonise the future in a way which ignores non-Western perspectives, histories, needs and priorities.

Feminist futures

Eleonora Masini, (1987) in writing about women as builders of the future, draws attention to the way in which the techno-industrial enterprise has also been one based entirely on masculinist values:

> Women are better adapted for the change from the industrial society to a new society, because women are not the carriers of the values of

the preceding industrial society. As they were not the builders of the future in the preceding society, they may become the builders of the future in a different society. As they were invisible in the industrial society, women may become visible and constructive in a post-industrial society.

Through early socialisation men and women in most societies are trained to view the world differently. In particular women are socialised into thinking more about human relationships and the social consequences of their actions. An extensive feminist literature is now available which reviews most aspects of the human endeavour, from ecology (Merchant, 1992) to the social construction of science (Harding, 1991).

Other researchers, such as Riane Eisler, (1990) have re-examined the historical and archaeological evidence of the past to offer new theories of cultural evolution. A male dominated hierarchical society began to emerge some 5000 years ago in Europe, before which a Goddess-worshipping, non-hierarchical and non-warring culture had existed for thousands of years. Eisler suggests two consequent models of cultural evolution: the Dominator Model, in which one half of society dominates the other, and the Partnership Model, in which men and women are equally valued and respected. Which will we choose for the future, she asks?

A rich literature also exists in women's science fiction and utopian writing. Both attest to the critical role that women have to play in creating more versatile and visionary scenarios for the future. Whilst science fiction has traditionally been seen as a male preserve, writers such as Sarah Lefanu (1988) have explored women's writing in this field and found an exciting fusion of feminist politics and the creative imagination. The radical possibilities of this form of writing are being used by women to explore possible futures in new and imaginative ways.

The long tradition of utopian literature in the West has also been invigorated by feminist perspectives. Nan Albinski's survey (1988) of women's utopias in British and American fiction reveals a wealth of writing from the nineteenth century onwards on themes pertaining to the nature of the good life and the good society. She describes the important change that occurred during the seventies:

> Utopia also changed around this time, lifted from the dystopian path in which it seemed to be set by the arrival of feminist writers, some

32

from the neighbouring genre of science fiction, which brings an infusion of optimism not equalled since the utopian golden age of the late nineteenth century. In numbers and in tone, they reflect the rise in feminism as the most important social movement of the 1970s, and their idealistic utopias are radically different from the continued dystopianism of male writers. Feminist writers also give dystopian warnings: frequently they offer the reader... both utopia and dystopia, so that each nightmare world is accompanied by its opposite.

Feminist writers are thus making a forceful contribution to the futures related literature, a contribution which needs to be given a much higher profile.

Summary

This chapter has drawn together three vital threads which will help educators better understand the significance of a futures perspective. It began by recognising that the future is increasingly a focus for popular concern in the face of rapid social, technological and environmental change. Attention was then drawn to the nature of the futures field and the importance of futures studies and examples given of some of the key concerns of futurists over the last twenty years.

The role of images of the future in relation to social and cultural change was emphasised and Polak's thesis that the rise and fall of societies is presaged by their images of the future. Positive guiding images of the future are currently lacking and we need to develop skills for envisioning preferable futures. During the course of the twentieth century images of the future have changed from utopian to dystopian.

Finally, it is essential to recognise and value widely differing perspectives on the future: much of the discourse on futures has a strong Western male bias and non-Western and feminist views of the future are vital. This sets the scene for the investigation that follows, into the research on how adults and young people view the future.

Chapter 3

Images of the Future

A major theme that emerged... was on conceptions of an uncompassionate future. Continued trends in depersonalisation, competitive pressures in schools and difficulties in finding work after leaving school... and a lack of genuinely loving or caring relationships were typically anticipated. Such imagery of the future was often coupled with expressions of helplessness about relentless, mechanistic change in which human feelings, self-esteem and aspirations are too readily sacrificed. — Frank Hutchinson

Despite the overwhelming importance of images of the future, relatively little research has been carried out on people's views of societal futures. Most of the research has taken the form of exploratory studies. David Livingstone (1976) comments:

The general importance of images of the future as mediating factors in social action has been postulated by... several scholars. Such theoretical work has not distinguished very clearly between hopes (what people want to see) and expectations (what they think will probably happen), or between people's attitudes regarding their personal future and their views on the societal future. There has been a substantial amount of empirical research on personal hopes and expectations. Such studies typically show no interest in discerning the

35

societal contexts people hope or expect to live in, but rather take the continuation of the present institutional context for granted.

This chapter reviews the existing research on adults' and young people's views of the future. It provides the background to, and sets the scene for, the UK study described in chapters 4 to 6.

Adult's views of the future

Some early studies

Bettina Huber (1978) suggests that the rapid pace of change in society may have a significant impact on how individuals view the future. She noted, however, that 'we know relatively little about this matter because social scientists rarely investigate images of the future'.

An interesting early study was by Kurt Danziger (1963) who invited four hundred South African students to write 'histories of the future.' They were asked to imagine themselves as historians in the twenty-first century looking back on events in South Africa and to write a short essay describing the major events that had occurred between 1960 and 2010. The essays were used to identify five differing orientations to the future. Thus Conservatives saw the future as being a return to the past, Catastrophists believed future events would destroy what was good in the present, whilst Liberals, Technicists and Revolutionaries all saw major improvements occurring in the future, but via different routes.

Each of the four social groups polled in the survey, Afrikaans, English, Indian and African, had a distinctively different view of South Africa's future. Not surprisingly, 46% of the African students saw the future in revolutionary terms, whilst 49% of Indians were liberal, 37% of Afrikaaners were technicist and 31% of English expected catastrophe. The individual's orientation to the future appeared to be a function of the way in which each experienced the relationship between rulers and ruled. Unfortunately Danziger did not say which of his respondents, if any, expected to see black majority rule in South Africa by 1994.

Hadley Cantril (1965) was responsible for another important early study. His Self-Anchoring Striving Scale enabled respondents to express their thoughts about the future in a way that allowed cross-cultural comparisons to be made. The scale is based on two questions which ask participants to describe the best and the worst possible future that they can imagine in ten to twenty years time. This is used to establish the upper and lower limits of a ten-point scale. Individuals are then asked to rate themselves and their country on this scale, their present position, their position five years ago, and their anticipated position in five years time. On a national level, hopes and fears can be compared depending on whether political, economic, social and other concerns are expressed.

This scale was used in fourteen different countries during the 1960s and Cantril summarises the overall findings as follows:

> It appears that people in the developed countries are fairly satisfied with the present and foresee limited progress in the future. In contrast, people in poorer countries are not particularly satisfied with the present and hope, as well as expect, that their situation will improve markedly in the future. This inter-country difference is reflected within nations too, in that persons of low socio-economic status are most likely to have aspirations for improving their situation in the years ahead.

Such differences were also apparent in an extensive cross-cultural study carried out in the late sixties called World Images 2000.

World Images 2000

Probably the largest and most authoritative investigation ever carried out in this field, its findings were published as *Images of the World in the Year 2000: A Comparative Ten Nation Study* (Ornauer et al., 1976). This major collaborative effort involved researchers in Britain, Norway, the Netherlands, Spain, Poland, Czechoslovakia, Yugoslavia, India and Japan. The questions asked of respondents were wide-ranging as the following examples indicate.

- Would you say that you think very much, much, little or not at all about the future of your country, not in a couple of years but, say, in the year 2000?

- How often would you say that you talk with somebody about the future of your country or the world?

- What do you think will be the difference between the year 2000 and today?

- What do you think will be the situation in your country by the year 2000? Do you think that people will be more happy or less happy than they are today?

In general terms the tendency to think, or to express thoughts, about the future was not very well developed amongst respondents. Images of the future often focused on likely developments in science and technology or concern about problems to do with war and peace, rather than the more broad social future. By and large, pessimistic visions of the future were better developed than optimistic visions. In the more developed nations there was a certain scepticism about science whereas in the less developed nations scientific development in any field was generally appreciated.

Johan Galtung (1976), in his conclusion, noted that:

> ... For the nations in our sample the future seems somehow to be synonymous with a technological future. The future is seen in technical terms, not in terms of culture, human enrichment, social equality, social justice, or in terms of international affairs... People may also think in terms of social future but regard it as unchangeable. But it seems more probable that they have only been trained to think technologically and have no other type of thoughts as a response to the stimulus 'future'; or at least have not been trained to express any other thoughts. And this will then become self-reinforcing since no one will be stimulated by others to think about social futures.

Particularly in the developed countries there was an association between pessimism, scientific scepticism and technological futures thinking.

Ontario Images 2000

In the early 1970s David Livingstone carried out a similar survey in Ontario, Canada. His starting point was that:

> Over the past decade, professional futurists and other intellectuals, as well as many expert-dominated public and private commissions, have engaged in ... efforts to envision probable or preferable futures for advanced industrial societies. Whether extrapolating present societal trends or stating a moral position on a particular sort of future, such efforts to construct long-term social policies have generally either

ignored or presumed the actual orientations to the future existing among the general public (Livingstone, 1976).

Livingstone (1983) was particularly concerned about the gap between the visions of the future held by intellectuals and the general public. His stress in the Ontario Images 2000 Project was on popular images of societal and educational futures. He wanted to investigate how often people thought about the future, how clear an image of the future they had, and the extent to which popular thinking was dominated by technological extrapolation.

A majority of respondents indicated frequent thinking about the future and Livingstone suggests that this marked a shift in interest in advanced capitalist societies since the earlier World Images 2000 Project. All classes indicated a high frequency of thinking about the future, especially corporate capitalists. Whilst fewer respondents claimed any great clarity about their images of the future, corporate capitalists, managers and professional employees claimed the most. The unemployed expressed the greatest future disorientation.

People were also asked how much influence they expected scientists and technologists to have in society by the year 2000. Over eighty percent of respondents expected them to have more or much more influence. Livingstone notes that this is 'only the most explicit of numerous indications of technological extrapolationist thinking' expressed in the survey. Respondents were also asked in both surveys about how much influence they themselves expected to have in public affairs. The majority of people in Ontario and the ten countries expected to have very little or no influence.

The two main differences observable in the later Ontario research are, firstly, that the frequency of thinking about the future appears to have increased and secondly that social problems are as likely to be the focus of people's images of the future as technological issues. The most general findings from the Ontario project were felt to be in accord with the Global Images 2000 Project.

[There is] a division of labour in nearly all human societies with regard to the future. All societies have elites, whose task is to be concerned with the future, and all societies have non-elites whose task is to challenge the elites but only at a superficial level and not on really fundamental issues. The fundamental issues are not presented as something wanted by the elite as a result of their vested interest — but as dictated by immutable social laws, even by natural laws ... Is it strange that populations, who are never really given a say when it comes to social future, start seeing social future as immutable and hence have a low level of future imagination? (Galtung, 1976).

No similar large-scale surveys have been carried out since these two projects. How popular images of the future may have changed in the last twenty years is thus something of an open question. However, anecdotal evidence suggests that lack of imaging capacity and foreclosure around pessimistic/technological images of the future is still the rule.

Young people's views of the future

As with adults the research on how young people view the future is scattered and of variable quality. Whilst the need to 'educate for the future' was first highlighted in the late sixties and early seventies, it is not until the eighties that serious consideration of young people's views began to emerge. There are now signs that such research may be about to enter a new and more critical phase.

Some early studies

In the early fifties James Gillespie and Gordon Allport (1955) carried out a survey of what young people in ten different countries felt about their individual and collective futures. The countries were the United States, New Zealand, South Africa, Egypt, Mexico, France, Italy, Germany, Japan and Israel. Two questions that the authors wanted to answer were: How does youth in various countries view the future? Do young people in different countries view their futures in essentially the same way? 'Our chief interest,' they wrote, 'is in the way the present dark and uncertain world situation affects youth's attitudes toward their personal lives and future careers'.

Gillespie and Allport asked students to write an autobiography of the future and to complete a questionnaire. The autobiography was entitled 'From now to 2000 AD' and participants were asked to write an essay of 1000 to 2000 words about their plans, expectations and aspirations for the future. The questionnaire included items on careers, family, travel, the best and worst things that could happen in the future, and the likelihood of war.

Amongst the similarities between countries was the importance of the family, an acceptance of moral standards, an interest in new developments in science and technology, a desire for greater racial equality, and fear of another world war. The national differences described seem very little to do with the future and more to do with the current culture and politics. Women generally wanted more freedom than most of the men respondents felt they should have. Amongst their conclusions the authors note that: 'Most youth regard war as needless and preventable. They are, however, pessimistic as to the possibility of avoiding a third world conflict'. With hindsight we can confirm Allport and Gillespie's speculation that, 'for all we know (attitudes) may reflect chiefly the political, economic and social situation prevailing at a given time'.

In his important book, *Learning For Tomorrow,* Alvin Toffler (1974) describes 'an unusual and confessedly non-scientific experiment' which he carried out with a class of 15-16 year olds. He asked them to write down and date seven events that they thought were likely to occur in the future. Collectively they described a disastrous future for the United States, including revolution, natural disasters and nuclear war. What troubled Toffler was that, whilst the students clearly found the future exciting, they also saw it as something impersonal, 'out there', not something they were involved in. By contrast, against this catalogue of global disasters, students wrote of their personal lives as a simple progression through work, marriage, success, retirement and death.

> No matter how turbulent a world they pictured, no matter how many new technologies might appear or what political revolutions might take place, the way of life foreseen for themselves as individuals seldom differed from the way of life possible in the present and actually lived by many today. It is as though they believed that everything happening outside one's life simply by-passes the individual. The respondents, in short, made no provision for change in themselves, no provision for adaptation to a world exploding with change (Toffler, 1974).

These findings, whilst somewhat anecdotal, still support the contention that each generation's view of the future is influenced by contemporary events. It also highlights a major dissonance between personal and global views of the future, something which remained an on-going theme in the literature for some time.

Studies in the 1980s

One of the first studies in the eighties was carried out by Mary Brown (1984) in Britain. It is noteworthy that this is the first piece of research to acknowledge that young people's views of the future are inextricably bound up with contemporary social change.

Brown sets the scene by comparing the values commonly expressed in the eighties with those of the seventies. In the latter decade, she notes, there was the beginning of a reaction against technological society, student revolt, the rise of the counter culture, the growth of the ecological movement. What, however, were the preoccupations of students in the eighties and what were their hopes and fears for the future?

In the first stage of the study two short essays were obtained from 250 16-18 year olds. The first was on how they would spend an ordinary day in the year 2000 and the second a description of the sort of future that they would like.

> From these essays certain common themes emerged. Of life in the future as expected: violence, unemployment, high technology, bore-dom, inflation, poverty, pollution, material prosperity, and, mainly from secondary modern girls, a life not much different from that of today. Of the future as desired, world peace was the most frequently mentioned ideal, and came into the vast majority of essays (Brown, 1984).

A large majority of the essays envisaged a highly technological future, although many students seemed uneasy about this. Non-materialistic values were expressed far more often than materialist ones and a 'disen-chantment with the modern, consumer society seemed to run through very many of the essays'.

As a result of factor analysis, twenty concerns were identified from the essays and used in the second stage of the study to create a questionnaire which was completed by over four hundred pupils. It asked them to state how likely or unlikely, on a five point scale, they thought twenty different items were by the year 2000, and how desirable each was. Amongst the items thought very likely or likely were advances in medicine (93%), major advances in technology (87%), high levels of unemployment (77%), and a leisure society (63%). Over half expected a nuclear disaster.

By contrast the items thought very desirable or desirable were advances in medicine (92%), stable prices and control of inflation (92%), conservation (87%), less pollution in the environment (79%) and greater prosperity for all (79%). Further factor analysis revealed four broad preferable futures which Brown labelled: Anomie (increased disorder), Easy Life (leisure society), Rural Paradise (countryside conservation), and Welfare (greater equality). Only a very small number wanted Anomie, mostly boys and those not taking exams. Many pupils, however, thought this future to be a likely one. Easy Life is 'the super industrial materialist future that politicians of all parties assume that we all want, and is the basis of industrialism and capitalism. These are the values that we are all assumed to hold by advertisers and by industry in general'. Whilst significantly more boys than girls wanted this, only a minority of the sample overall wanted this future. Girls, more than boys, generally rejected a technological future in preferring the Rural Paradise scenario.

The most popular scenario was Welfare which, although very different from Rural Paradise, is still non-materialist. It consisted of three items: greater equality in society, assistance for Third World countries, and advances in medicine. This also was far more popular with girls. Brown points out that her samples are not representative and that any conclusions are tentative. However, even a cautious interpretation, she suggests, 'indicates that the majority of these young people are not greatly in favour of our technological society'. There was a general pessimism about the future and also distinct gender differences. 'We live in a male-dominated society and the materialistic values it proclaims seem to be endorsed by and large by young males. Young females seem to have other values and different outlooks and desires for the future.'

There are other ways of finding about about children's views of the future which can arise out of everyday classroom work. Thus Cathie Holden, (1989) working with a class of 9-10 year olds, asked them to draw their probable and preferable timelines for the future. She comments:

The children's perceptions of a preferable future indicated preoccupations which surprised me and to which we were to return again and again in the follow-up work. Although they did want 'new toys', 'no telling off' and 'different sweets', they also showed a common concern for an end to poverty and crime ('no murders', 'no more muggings') and an end to war. Interestingly, out of all the timelines produced by the class, none expected nuclear war in their own lifetime — some saw it afterwards or in the very distant future or not at all. A sign that children are more optimistic than adults? But the fact that all the timelines featured an end to war in their preferable futures, does show children's great concerns in this area — nine-year olds are not as innocent as some would have us believe (Holden, 1989).

The reference to nuclear war marks another specific change in children's perceptions of the future. As the arms race escalated during the 1980s the fear of nuclear war became a major preoccupation in many countries. A number of studies established that this fear also extended to young people (Beardslee and Mack, 1982). These studies were essentially about young people's nuclear fears, although sometimes set within the broader context of their perceptions of war and peace. Such research represents a specialised case of the wider views of the future considered in this chapter.

As discussed in chapter 2, the nuclear arms race helped to create popular images of the future which were extremely dystopian. One review of the research (Educators for Social Responsibility, 1982) suggested that most children were aware of the nuclear arms race by the end of primary school and that they felt betrayed by adults who had let this possibility come about. Adolescents felt they had the most to lose, because they were just beginning to think about their personal futures only to be faced by images of extinction. It was suggested that this uncertainty about the future might, in some cases, affect normal developmental processes, in helping to create a 'live for today' philosophy and a turning away from adult authority.

Lynell Johnson (1987) describes a national survey carried out in the United States. A questionnaire was completed by more than 600,000 students at primary and secondary level and findings taken from a randomly selected sample of 140,000 students. Questions were divided into three categories, those dealing with the student's own future, the future of the United States, and the future of the world. The future was defined as 'when you are as old as your parents are now'.

Most students had a conventional, but optimistic, view of their own personal futures. The great majority expected to be married with children, to own a home and a car, to be richer than their parents, and happier than they are now. Boys and girls showed an equal increase in awareness of the need for gender equity with age. Overall 'the picture that emerges is of a traditional lifestyle — with the exception of some evidence on changing sex roles — in a bright personal future'.

Students' views of the future of the United States were less optimistic. More than half believed that drug abuse and crime would become more serious, and 40 percent felt unemployment, the national debt and poverty would get worse. When considering various economic and social problems facing the country as a whole, most predicted either no improvement or a deteriorating situation. When asked which changes they would most like to see happen, sexual equality was ranked first by both boys and girls. In this case, but not in others, their probable and preferable futures were the same.

Students' views of the future of the world were even less optimistic. Sixty percent felt that the danger of nuclear war would increase and almost as many saw depletion of natural resources and pollution of air, land and water getting worse. Half felt that there would be increasing problems over world population and food supply. The only problem area they saw hope for was in improvement in race relations.

'Perhaps the most striking finding of all,' says Johnson, 'is the discrepancy, or set of discrepancies, between these youngsters' views of their personal futures and their views of the futures of the United States and the world'. A teacher colleague who had taught futures studies courses for fifteen years, pointed out to him that this discrepancy is the one he encountered most consistently amongst his own students.

It is useful to consider comments made by Noel Gough (1988b) in his review of research on children's images of the future. In particular he queries the assumptions brought by the researchers themselves to such work.

> For the most part, they seek to demonstrate that children's pessimism is the product of some form of adult culpability, usually an intellectual or moral deficiency in the education system or the popular media. Moreover, like the majority of scientific investigations, the research is invariably designed to produce the desired or expected results.

Thus, he points out, some researchers feel children's anxieties about developments in science and technology are groundless and arise merely from lack of knowledge or inadequate teaching. The blame for that ignorance is directed at what they consider to be unnecessarily alarmist teachers involved in social education, environmental education, development education and peace studies. Gough also argues that many of the techniques used for eliciting information from children are very obtrusive and thus may encourage the pessimistic responses that researchers expect to find.

Kay Boyer (1989) carried out a study which attempted to draw together existing social theory on the future, images of the future in children's literature, and English teaching. She was particularly interested in whether children's literature on futures themes could be used to explore critically social and political issues. Most of the images of the future in the books she reviewed were pessimistic, focusing on the hazards of technology or ecological disaster.

She worked with four English classes of 13-14 year olds and asked them to write about 'A day in someone's life in the year 2020'. Pupils were asked to make clear which features of their scenarios they felt were good and which bad. Most commonly these descriptions portrayed an optimistic high-tech view of the future. Classroom observation showed that although the study of such texts helped to develop literacy skills it did not lead to critical questioning of the described alternative futures. Boyer claimed a cathartic role for such literature in exploring children's fears for the future but the evidence for this was limited.

Studies in the 1990s

At the beginning of this decade the Henley Centre for Forecasting (1991) published a report on children's visions of the future environment. The survey looked in detail at the attitudes of 10-14 year olds and revealed a high level of interest in environmental issues, something seen by children not as radical but rather as common sense. Three main sorts of concern were identified: global issues such as deforestation, the ozone layer, global warming; issues closer to home such as litter, pollution, car emissions; and issues related to animals, especially vivisection and endangered species.

Local issues were mentioned much less than global ones, about which children generally appeared to show a high level of understanding. Their visions of the future tended to be somewhat apocalyptic so, not surprisingly, a high degree of helplessness was expressed. The required action for the future was felt to be a modification of patterns of consumption rather than any need for major changes in Western lifestyles. The main conclusions of the study are that children take environmental problems very seriously but are generally pessimistic about the future.

> When asked to draw their image of the environment in a hundred years' time, not one came up with a positive vision. There were no pictures of a sanitised sci-fi world. Almost all the applications of science (apart from the occasional solar powered car) were ones which were deliberately harsh and inhuman — robotic sheep, for example. Certainly none of them could envisage a time when all our environmental problems are solved. At best, there was a belief that we would come to our senses just before the point of no return (Henley Centre, 1991).

Josiah Dodds and Lin Chong-de (1992) explored the future concerns held by teenagers in Beijing. Drawn from Grades 7-12, some 1800 students participated in their questionnaire. Over-population of the planet was ranked as the most serious concern, followed by environmental pollution, and personal concerns such poor grades, not finding a satisfying job and a parent dying. Fear of nuclear war, a particular interest of the researchers, was ranked seventh.

Comparing their findings with other research, the authors note that Chinese teenagers were much more pessimistic about the likelihood of nuclear war than their American or Soviet counterparts. If this concern sounds dated it is because it was actually carried out in the late eighties. They note that teenagers' concerns for the future probably reflect current issues and that this will change over time. 'The findings of this study suggest that teenagers' concerns can be a good index of a country's current social, political, economic, and environmental problems.'

The work previously described by Gillespie and Allport (1955) has since been replicated in the United States three times. The most recent of these time-lag studies is reported by Douglas Kleiber, Wayne Major and Guy Manaster (1993). The most significant finding of the study was that students now appeared less conservative than their 1982 counterparts, although they were still more conservative than the students of 1971. An apparent increase in activism was noted amongst students, approaching the levels found in the 1970s.

The authors conclude that:

> Whereas the personal outlook for the future of 1992 students must be regarded as generally positive, their views of world affairs indicate a mixed picture. Attitudes towards international affairs and reduced concerns about the threats of war reflect some of the ease from previous 'cold war' tensions. But 1992 students show a continuing and disturbing trend toward lower expectation of racial equality and are in this sense less optimistic than students from the previous two decades (Kleiber et al., 1993).

A follow-up to the US survey described by Johnson (1987) was carried out by the journal *Weekly Reader* (1993) which analysed responses from 56,000 Grade 2 to 6 children. A dramatic increase was noted in the number who felt they would continue to live in their home community rather than move away. This was thought to reflect the decreasing mobility of the US population generally. Children look forward to being high-order consumers and have an optimistic view of their economic future, not necessarily consonant with current economic indicators. A majority expect to be happier in the future than today. At the same time they expect unemployment, poverty, crime and drugs to be more serious problems in the US than today.

One recent study is by Richard Eckersley (1994), who notes that whilst earlier studies often focused on concerns about nuclear war, more recent research shows that 'young people's sense of futurelessness has not lessened with the end of the cold war. Rather the studies suggest that a deepening concern not only about war, but also global environmental destruction, growing violence and inequality, and an increasingly dehumanised, machine dominated world'.

Frank Hutchinson's doctoral thesis (1992) represents one of the most detailed studies so far of young people's views of the future. His study was of Australian teenagers but many of the themes that emerge resonate with similar work from North America and Europe. He used a questionnaire with 650 upper secondary school students and follow-up dialogue in small groups with a sample of the respondents.

In relation to the students' images of feared future worlds he writes:

> Many of the young people in this study expressed a strong sense of negativity, helplessness, despondency and even anguish about the anticipated problems facing their society and the world at large. For a majority, negative imagery of the future ranged from perceptions of intensifying pressure and competition in schools in the twenty-first century to worsening trends in physical violence and war, joblessness and poverty, destructive technology and environmental degradation (Hutchinson, 1993).

Amongst these concerns six major themes could be identified: i) an uncompassionate world, depersonalised and uncaring; ii) a physically violent world, with a high likelihood of war; iii) a divided world, between the 'haves' and the 'have nots'; iv) a mechanised world, of violent technological change; v) an environmentally unsustainable world, with continued degradation of the biosphere; vi) a politically corrupt and deceitful world, where voting is a waste of time.

Hutchinson was equally concerned, however, to explore young people's images of preferable future worlds and he found that they fell into four broad categories. These were: i) technocratic dreaming, in which students uncritically accept technofix solutions for all problems (most popular amongst boys); ii) a demilitarisation and greening of science and technology, to meet genuine human needs; iii) intergenerational equity, accepting responsibilities also for the needs of future generations; iv) making peace with people and planet, via a reconceptualisation of ethics and also of lifestyles.

The value of Hutchinson's study lies in its attention to detail, its sensitivity to young people themselves, and its location within a broader body of research on the educational and cultural implications of such findings. It is this sort of research that is of most use to educators rather than simple attitude surveys.

Review of the research

Adult's views

Although the research reviewed here has been somewhat limited, it has improved over the years in depth and quality. Several useful techniques have been evolved, such as essays on future history as used by Danziger, Cantril's Self-Anchoring Striving Scale, or the detailed questionnaires used in the ten-nation study. Certainly there has been an increase in sophistication from the early studies, and the World 2000 and Ontario projects represent a high watermark in this research. They also came at a time when futures studies was in the ascendant. Perhaps the absence of comparable studies since then reflects the decline of serious interest in futures noted in chapter 2.

Generally the tendency to think about the broader future seems poorly developed amongst adults and, when it does occur, is often locked by default into a narrowly scientific and technological focus. It is as if the only conceivable future is one controlled by science and technology, whether for good or bad. It is not surprising that people often feel they have little control over the future and are more likely to envisage pessimistic futures than optimistic ones.

Young people's views

More research has been carried out on young people's views of the future than those of adults. One wonders if this is a convenient distancing of the problem from the adult mind, i.e. it matters more what children think about the future of the planet than what adults think. The issue is conveniently placed on the shoulders of the future rather than the present generation.

It is clear from the studies described here that perceptions of the future vary in several significant ways over time, while also expressing increasingly common concerns. Images of the future come across as far less concrete in Gillespie and Allport's study in the 50s. Toffler, reporting on the late 60s and early 70s, was one of the first to note the dissonance between personal future optimism and global pessimism. Brown, in the 80s, is able to see more clearly how students' attitudes and values vary with the confronting issues of the time; the research on nuclear fears is a primary example. Johnson picks up again the need to differentiate between personal, national and global futures. In the 90s the Henley Centre and others note the primacy of environmental concerns.

There is also a difference between the time-lag studies of Kleiber and those of researchers such as Hutchinson. The former focus on student attitudes and values via their concerns for the future, whereas the latter focuses more directly on the notion of futures itself. Hutchinson's work not only acts as a summation of much that has gone before, with its emphasis on young people's anguish, but also points the way forward in highlighting the need to explore more explicitly images of both feared and desired futures.

Summary

This chapter reviewed a representative sample of the research on both adults' and young people's views of the future. Such views relate strongly to the social and political issues of the time. Whilst these have varied somewhat in detail, the general trend since the 1960s has been towards an increasing concern about the future of society and the planet. Images have become increasingly pessimistic and now embrace a wide range of issues. The research thus supports the broad picture, set out in the previous chapter, of the changing nature of such images during the course of the twentieth century.

Images of the future in the western world often hinge narrowly around scientific and technological developments, sometimes seen as beneficial but more often as dystopian. It is as if science and technology have a life of their own which the ordinary citizen feels she can neither understand nor control. In the face of such fears it is increasingly important to focus on people's images of preferred futures. If they can be elaborated and envisioned more clearly then perhaps they can provide the basis for creating a more just and sustainable future.

PART TWO — VISIONS OF THE FUTURE

The survey

The chapters in Part Two of this book are based on a survey carried out by the authors in 1994 on young people's views of the future. The first survey of its kind in the UK for a decade, it drew on the findings of previous research in its focus and its design. The aim was to find out what children are thinking about the future in the 1990s and to explore the views of children at different stages in their education. Information on the perspectives of children from ages 7 to 18 would clarify how young people's views change over time, and have implications for futures education in both primary and secondary schools. The study drew on the work of Ornauer et al (1976) but breaks new ground by taking a developmental perspective across a ten year age span.

The study began by investigating how often children think, talk and read about the future. This was then explored at a personal, local and global level, since research has indicated that there are often clear distinctions between these perspectives (Toffler, 1974). Whilst Johnson (1987) focused on the personal, the national and the world, it was felt that for this survey, young people's views about their local area would be more valuable and might produce more divergent answers than questions about the UK. These three levels of personal, local and global run throughout the survey.

A second focus was on the hopes and fears of young people, an aspect also previously researched by Brown (1984) and others. Children were asked to write freely on three major hopes for their personal future, the future of their local area and the future of the world. Then they did this for their fears. The open-ended nature of these questions allowed for a greater variety of responses and depth than closed questions. These responses were illuminated by further questions on particular issues such as pollution, unemployment, violence, families, women and poverty.

Pupils were offered four different future scenarios to consider (Hicks, 1994). These were: Same as Today (a future very similar to today with the same sorts of problems and solutions); New Technology (many problems solved by new developments in science and technology); Global Disaster (increase in global poverty and environmental damage) and Environmental Concern (a changed world due to increased environmental awareness). Pupils were asked to rank these in the order in which they would most *prefer* them to come about and then in the order in which they felt they were most *likely* to come about.

Finally the survey focused on possible action by young people and by schools to create a better future. This gave respondents a chance to say what they did, if anything, about the issues under discussion, what their school did and what they thought their schools *should* do. This was discussed in subsequent interviews.

Nearly four hundred pupils were involved in all, from eight schools in the south-west: four primary and four secondary. Two age groups were sampled in each: years 2 and 6 in primary schools (ages 6-7 and 10-11) and years 9 and 13 in secondary schools (ages 13-14 and 17-18).These groups correlate with National Curriculum testing ages and provided views from children at key stages in their education. For clarity, the children in the text are referred to as age 7 (year 2), age 11 (year 6), age 14 (year 9) and age 18 (year 13).

To ensure a representative sample, schools were chosen from a cross-section of urban and rural environments and a variety of socio-economic backgrounds. Two of the schools were inner-city and multi-ethnic to ensure that the views of white, black and Asian children were heard. A small group of children from each class was interviewed after completing the questionnaires, to examine some of their responses in greater depth.

Chapter 4

Primary school pupils

I have often thought about the world and how I would like it to be. I have thought about helping people like the RSPCA, WWF, RSPB, Children in Need. I have thought about doing my own club and I used to make bins and put them around and it did work. When I saw poor people on the streets they had a sign saying: 'Hungry and helpless. Please put some money in my hat. PS I really need it.' I put in £1.50 with my own pocket money. — Girl, aged 11

Personal futures

To ascertain the level of interest primary school children show in their personal future, they were asked how often they thought about this and how often they talked about it with friends. Half the 7 year olds claim to think about their future often, almost twice as many girls as boys saying so. The 11 year old children claim to think about the future slightly less often than the younger children, and only one third say they talk about it with friends. Three quarters of all primary school children are optimistic that their life in the future will be better, although some voice concerns.

I'm worried about living like a tramp and can I trust any persons to help me? (girl, 7)

I'd like to be well-off or middle class. I hope not to be influenced by drugs and cigarettes (boy, 11).

Regardless of the area they live in, children in both age groups hope for a future characterised by a good job or material well being. There are very few examples of children hoping for a fantasy future: most are concerned with establishing themselves in the adult world. Their hopes centre around jobs, housing, doing well at school and establishing relationships with a partner and having children. They see good health as important.

Tables 4.1 and 4.2 show important variations by age and gender. Children at the end of primary school have a greater concern for a good

Table 4.1 Personal hopes for future (ages 7 and 11)					
	Age 7		Age 11		Primary total
	girls	boys	girls	boys	
Good life	35	36	52	74	49
Employment	26	32	48	61	42
Relationships	28	5	45	20	25
Education	2	0	26	22	13
Health	9	3	18	22	13

(percentage of children mentioning these hopes)
Note: Because children could name as many hopes or fears as they wished, the numbers in tables 4.1-6 add up to more than 100%.

Table 4.2 Personal fears for future (ages 7 and 11)					
	Age 7		Age 11		Primary total
	girls	boys	girls	boys	
Health problems	62	30	43	42	44
Violence	15	17	30	36	25
No money	8	13	33	25	20
No/poor job	0	0	33	39	18
Family problems	23	13	17	14	17

(percentage of children mentioning these fears)

education than younger children; likewise the desire for a good job increases with age — as does awareness of health issues.

7 year olds

Younger children's hopes are often immediate, related to the things they would like now rather than things they might like later as adults. They reveal differing levels of ability in conceptualising the future. There is the emergence of an ability to think ahead, and with it the realisation that life in the future may be something to work towards as well as something to be concerned about. Asked about their hopes for the future, some 7 year olds want 'sunny weather' or 'three cats and two guinea pigs', whereas others can begin to envisage themselves as adults. One writes: 'I hope I have long dresses' and another already has a vision of her intended caring role: 'I will be kind... help people who are lonely... help people who are blind'.

The fears of these young children for their personal future often mirror their hopes. Their main concerns centre around their families, and around having no money or poor health. They also express concern about being attacked by animals, about fires in the house and burglars. Reality and fantasy often sit side by side. The children have not yet managed to sort out what is probable in the future and what the world of make-believe. On the one hand we get those who worry about 'having naughty children' or:

> I hope I don't get too many babies, because you haven't got as much money... and pets as well.

And on the other, concerns about:

> A bear eating me. Fighting a dinosaur.

> Different kinds of animals that might attack you, like lions and wart-hogs.

These concerns are obviously very real to children and one wonders how often they are given the chance to discuss such hopes and fears in school.

11 year olds

The difference between 7 and 11 year olds is significant. The older children are more rooted in the impending world of the adult and their hopes and concerns are closer to those of secondary school pupils. For 11 year olds, a good education is seen as important and a good job is something that two thirds of the boys see as desirable. Future hopes also envisage the good life, especially for boys: 'I'd like to have a luxury home with a swimming pool and a spa and a blend-in ski slope and ice-skating rink'. For other children, especially girls, relationships are also important. One girl hopes for 'a nice kind husband' and another hopes to 'live with my dad... that my mum and her boyfriend split up... '.

Despite the materialistic desires of the boy above, the majority of children have a well-developed sense of responsibility.

I hope to be famous but not to be richly dressed but to give lots to poor children and people who starve and are humble. That my children like school and are very interesting and kind to others (boy, 11).

I hope to travel the earth. I want to help save the earth (girl, 11).

As with the youngest children, the fears of 11 year olds largely mirror their hopes. A third mention unemployment as a fear and a third mention lack of money, i.e. the inability to obtain the good life. Ill-health emerges as a concern for 40% of the children: a girl worries that 'I will die young... that I might get cancer... that I might start smoking'. A third mention homelessness:

I'm worried that we may be split up and go somewhere else. We might get kicked onto the streets and have nowhere to go (boy, 11).

While younger children are worried about monsters and animals attacking them, children of 11 are more aware of the risks of mugging or rape. One girl put her fears succinctly: 'to be killed, to be hurt, to be raped'. A third of both boys and girls are concerned about being the object of violence. At this age they are beginning to extend their boundaries in terms of personal play space and walking to and from school but they are still physically small and unable to defend themselves.

Local futures

Interest in the future of their local area seems low among primary school children, with less than a quarter claiming to think or talk about it often. Boys appear less interested than girls, with a third more boys saying they 'never' think or talk about it. Local newspapers do not feature much in their reading habits and they show little interest in regional television news. However, when asked to write about their hopes and fears for their local area, a high degree of interest actually emerges.

7 year olds

For the youngest children, there is a concern that their local area may be subject to the violence they see in other places on TV. As with their personal future, children of 7 exhibit the same combination of fantasy and knowledge about real events.

> I hope people don't come and start fighting here like in other countries... like in India and Bosnia.

> If they did I'd be OK. I've got a sword.

Although some of their ideas are dominated by fantasy, they show an awareness of social and environmental conditions and are generally optimistic that the future will be better. More than two-thirds of 7 year olds feel there will be less pollution in their local area in the future. People will have more knowledge and try to improve the environment.

> People will try and stop the pollution and throw them in the bin for recycling.

> They will get better inventions... they will get batteries so they don't use exhausts for cars.

Those that disagree cite their own experience:

> It's getting worse and worse because they have discovered coca-cola bottles in the river... it's pollution.

A similar pattern emerges when asking children whether there will be more or less poverty in their community. Seven year olds are optimistic: only a fifth think there will be more poverty in their local area; 60% believe things will get better.

The children's comments reveal that for them poverty is a result of unemployment, ill-health and growing older. They also associate it with homelessness.

My dad can't work because he's allergic to things... to car fumes.

I saw some poor people in London when we were crossing a bridge and they were living in boxes... They just get cold and then they die.

In other schools children are more optimistic. One child thinks there will be 'more jobs and if you get jobs you get paid' and another says that there will be 'less poor people because there'll be more builders to make more houses'.

11 year olds

The·hopes and fears of 11 year old children are reflected in concern for the prosperity of their local area and less crime, against both property and people. Over half are concerned about pollution and want to see increased facilities for recycling, less pollution from factories and less litter.
The 11 year olds' fears directly mirror their hopes, showing real concern that and crime might increase and that conditions could lead to urban degeneration.

I want racism, bullying, violence and drunkenness to stop.

I'm afraid of it being knocked down. Burning down. More homeless people.

Table 4.3 Hopes for local area (age 11)			
	Age 11		Total
	girls	boys	
Less pollution	53	59	56
Better amenities	36	35	36
Less crime	32	28	30
Prosperity	30	20	25
Less traffic	15	35	25
(percentage of children mentioning these hopes)			

Table 4.4 Fears for local area (age 11)			
	Age 11		Primary total
	girls	boys	
More crime	44	38	41
More pollution	36	35	36
Terrorism	23	35	29
Unemployment	22	21	22
Homelessness	18	0	9
(percentage of children mentioning these fears)			

Along with a desire for greater prosperity for the area often comes a plea for more amenities. This ranges from a desire for 'more bins, more hospitals, more hostels' to 'more playing areas and shops' and leisure facilities for young people. One girl expresses her hope that facilities for disabled people will be improved and another wants 'more soup kitchens and homes for the homeless'. Traffic is also a major concern, especially for the boys. Over a third of the boys mention less traffic as something they would like, and say that they want:

> No more road works. Have traffic lights in every road. Have more bike cycle routes.

11 year old children mention two fears not mentioned by the responses of the secondary school children. They are aware of natural disasters occurring in other countries (floods, earthquakes) and a third of the boys worry that similar disasters might happen here. Fewer girls are worried, but one girl asks whether she will know when 'global warming will make it flood here: will someone tell me in time to get out?' Linked to this is a fear of terrorism. One boy dreads his town being bombed and there are numerous mentions of the IRA and the possibility of violence in their area. Children also mention the war in Bosnia and are worried that it could spread to their locality.

Eleven year olds are less positive than younger children about pollution being reduced in the future. Half think there will be more pollution and about a third think it will be the same. For them, pollution is related to factory emissions, car exhausts, the need for clean air and the need to recycle things. There is a growing awareness amongst 11 year olds that the issues are complex and that one solution might only elicit another set of problems.

> I've been to the recycling centre and they make pollution burning it all...I saw loads of smoke coming out of the chimney... ...they kept on going with trucks dumping it into the fire, ...That's what's causing a hole in the ozone layer.

One boy suggests that scientists will be forced to find alternative energy sources because 'in 50 years from now we'll be running out of petrol and major resources like that'. The consensus is that this will also have to be 'ozone friendly'. The children feel this to be a major issue which will affect their future and they want more information about it.

The 11 year olds are equally divided about whether poverty in their local area will be more, the same or less . Poverty is seen as linked to unemployment, and, as with the debate on pollution, there is an awareness that the issues are complex. Increased technology may mean increased poverty for some because it will mean fewer jobs, but increased indus-trialisation could also create jobs.

Whereas children of 7 have no notion of how to improve the quality of life, the 11 year olds show an emerging awareness of the power of government and the possibility of greater equity. One girl offers this solution for alleviating poverty:

> If we didn't have money, people could have ration cards, The more you work the more you'd get on your ration card. If you're lazy, you wouldn't get any. If you clean your home, sweeping, you'd get more.

One boy concludes:

> It's hard to get a job, I'll probably move away when I'm grown up. My brother's gone to America.

Children are concerned about the levels of crime and violence in their local area. Two-thirds think this will get worse in the future. They relate the presence of violence to unemployment, lack of police action, drunk driving and a decreasing supply of resources.

At the rate we're going... if there's more unemployment there will be more violence... They're dead bored and they have no jobs... If there's a bad environment and natural resources are dropping, people will have to pay more for water and they'll have less money, so there'll be more fighting.

This boy's attempt to grapple with the complexities of the issues indicates the attempts children of this age are making to try and understand the world they see around them.

By contrast, racial prejudice is an issue children feel they can do something about. Two schools provide an interesting contrast. In one mainly white, affluent city school, the children have been covering aspects of discrimination and prejudice in their Religious Education programme. This has obviously had a great impact and they feel that there will be less prejudice in the future because of what they have learnt.

I don't think racism will go up because I think people have learnt their lesson... When people shot Martin Luther King everybody thought 'that's not very nice is it?', because he was quite nice actually.

Yes, so was Mahatma Gandhi.

They assume that all children will have learnt what they had learnt at school, which will help towards the eradication of racism. One boy adds:

Perhaps someone might become the manager of a company and not judge someone by how they behave and what they look like, because they've learnt about it (prejudice) at school.

Black and Asian children in another city do not share this optimism. They think racism is getting worse and are not optimistic about the situation improving:

Some of my relatives, I want them to move, they get racist attacks... It's my auntie, they're going to burn her house down, and my little cousin, he won't go to sleep. They did tell the police but one of my cousins, he got hurt and all the white people was on the boy's side that pushed my cousin and he was crying.

The children say that school is alright because only 'some people' are racist. A girl explains that 'they call you Paki, but we don't mind because it just means clean and beautiful...' They feel that prejudice will not lessen

65

Figure 4.1: Work on prejudice (age 11)

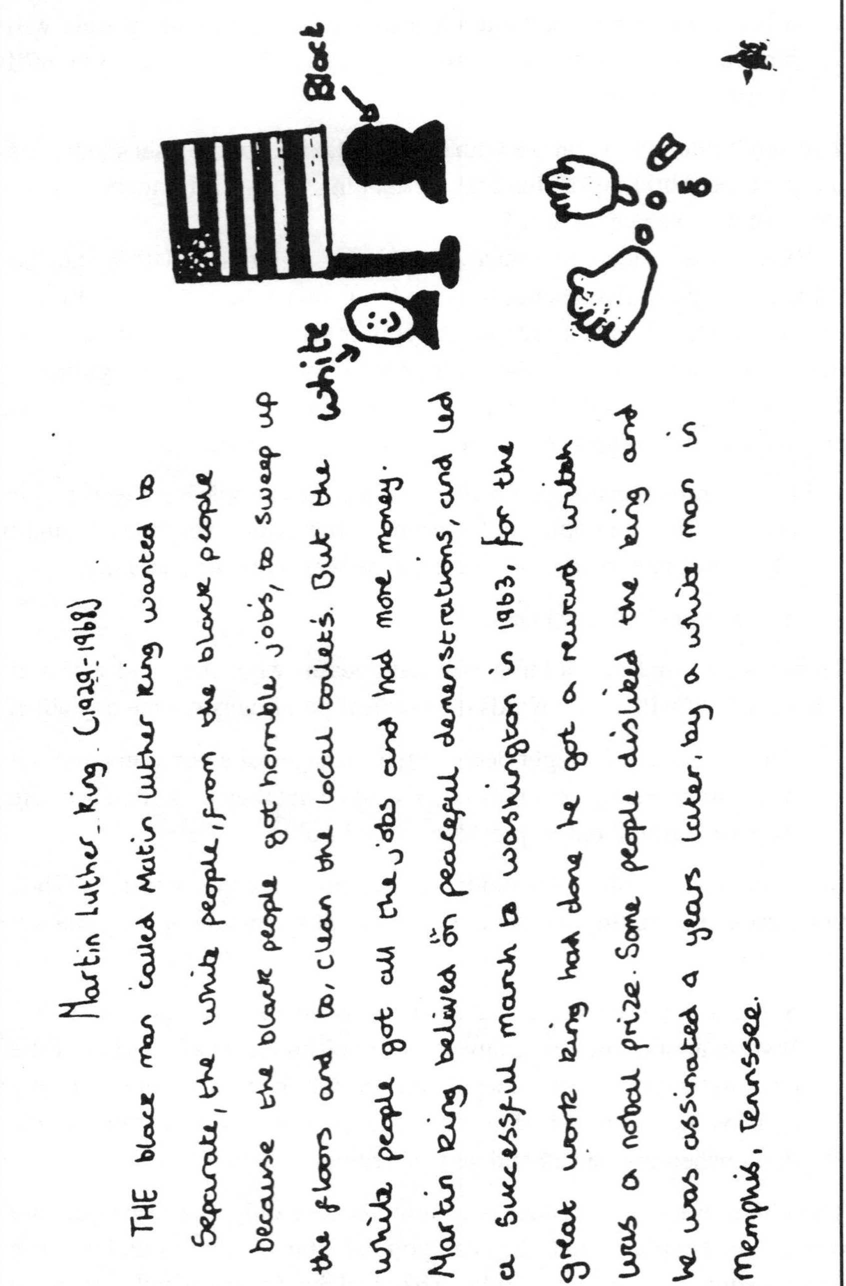

Martin luther king (1929-1968)

THE black man called Matin luther king wanted to separate, the white people, from the black people because the black people got horrible jobs, to sweep up the floors and to, clean the local toilets. But the white people got all the jobs and had more money. Martin King believed in peaceful demonstrations, and led a successful march to washington in 1963, for the great work king had done he got a reward which was a nobal prize. Some people disliked the king and he was assinated a years later, by a white man in Memphis, Tennssee.

in other areas either, and are very vehement that it is much worse in London and will be even more so in the future. They see the situation improving 'depending on the people who make the rules, like the president and that'. They cannot recall learning about issues to do with prejudice at school but feel strongly that it should be discussed.

Global Futures

Interest in the future of the world appears to be high, with 41% of 7 year olds thinking about it often and one-third sometimes: Girls are more interested than boys. For children at the end of their primary education, nearly two-thirds often think about global issues. Nearly half of 11 year olds acknowledge that they often see something on television about the world's future, although they read and talk about it much less. Whereas both 7 and 11 year olds say their own life in the future will be better, only the younger children are optimistic about life improving for other people.

7 year olds

Pollution emerges as a concern again and the younger children are not optimistic about global pollution decreasing. One 7 year old boy thinks oil tankers will make pollution worse in the future because:

> When they deliver the oil to the country, when they go back they wash their tanks out and all the oil comes out and when the birds want fish they go into the sea and the birds and the fish are polluted and they die.

Table 4.5 Hopes for global future (ages 7 and 11)					
	Age 7		Age 11		Primary total
	girls	boys	girls	boys	
No war/peace	17	26	77	74	49
Less pollution	29	50	55	47	45
Food/no poverty	29	11	45	42	32
Good relationships	15	20	19	23	19
(percentage of children mentioning these hopes)					

Table 4.6 Fears for global future (ages 7 and 11)					
	Age 7		Age 11		Primary totals
	girls	boys	girls	boys	
Disasters	55	82	19	29	46
War	0	12	54	72	35
Pollution	0	18	47	14	20
Poverty/no food	10	0	26	32	17
(percentage of children mentioning these fears)					

Another adds:

> I wish there would be no more war or pollution...because it will pollute the air and we'll be breathing in bad air and it will kill us.

On a rather plaintive note one girl admits she put 'yes' to less pollution because 'I like the world so much' and another adds philosophically, 'I hope it's better... but it might be worse... we don't know'.

Children of 7 are not optimistic about the alleviation of global poverty either. Nearly half think there will be more poor people. Children are aware of poverty in other countries and in their own community.

> It's in Barbados, Africa, Caribbean, Jamaica, India... And it's the same in Bristol... it's all around the world. I see people begging; they sit there on the floor. And some people do something for their money... they sing.

A boy from another school adds:

> I think there will be more countries splitting up so there will be more poor people... like Russia.

While war is cited as a fear by a minority of 7 year olds, most of the boys regard global disaster as an issue. They talk about 'the world blowing up', the world 'exploding', or aliens invading and killing all the people. The mixture of reality and fantasy seen earlier in their fears for the personal future and that of their local area is found again in their visions of the global future.

11 year olds

Children of 11 follow the same pattern as the younger ones in being pessimistic about the chances of improvement in the global situation. However, they are even more pessimistic: two-thirds think there will be more pollution, 77% of the boys and 55% of the girls. Examples of global pollution are 'the pollution that comes from tankers, from oil slicks' and a belief that:

> It'll be worse because of people chopping down trees and the ozone layer is getting worse. They should close down some factories.

Eleven year olds are equally divided about the possibility of poverty being alleviated in their local area. Nearly half think there will be more poverty globally, and a third think life will be much the same. As with the discussion on local poverty they show an awareness that it is closely linked to unemployment and that new technology may create opportunities as well as job losses.

Three-quarters of 11 year olds identify the threat of war as one of their chief concerns. Two-thirds expect the world to be more violent in the future and the images they have of other countries often involve violence and war. The children's understanding of distant places appears to be influenced by the media.

> It (violence) will get worse because I think other people from other countries will come over and there'll be lots of fighting ...There's a lot of crime in America and they might come over here.

The desire for good relationships between countries, mentioned in their hopes, is perhaps a corollary to the absence of war. Children hope for people to 'get on together', that 'white and black people will be friends' and for an end to violence.

> I hope that there will not be homeless people and no wars or no people like the people in Bosnia.

> There will be no more hunger. No more wars and fighting. No more killing and crime and also animals set free from zoos.

There is very little difference in the views of boys and girls — they appear to share such concerns equally and feel equally powerless about them.

Visions of the future

Choice of scenarios

The children were presented with four possible scenarios for the future, as described below.

Table 4.7 Four scenarios for the future

Same as today
In this future not much will have changed. Life will be very similar to today with the same sorts of problems and similar sorts of solutions. Life will really be very much like it is today.

New technology
In this futire there will be many new developments in science and technology which will solve many problems, e.g. space travel, intelligent robots, more nuclear power and breakthroughs in medicine and health.

Global disaster
In this future life will be much worse than today. There may be an increase in world hunger, damage to the environment, flooding as a result of global warming or more wars in different parts of the world.

Environmental concern.
In this future many people have changed the way that they think about the planet and its people. There will be more emphasis on taking care of the environment and taking care of other people.

The 7 year olds were also provided with drawings of the scenarios and asked to number them in the order they would most like them to come about, i.e. as preferable futures.

Table 4.8 Preferred scenarios (ages 7 & 11)

	Age 7		Age 11		Primary
	girls	boys	girls	boys	Total
Environmental concern	35	35	73	55	50
Same as today	36	45	16	13	28
New technology	27	13	10	32	21
Global disaster	0	7	0	0	2

(percentage of children putting each scenario first)

Table 4.9 Expected scenarios (age 11)

	Age 11		Primary
	girls	boys	Total
Same as today	40	32	36
New technology	24	30	27
Global disaster	19	28	24
Environmental concern	16	11	14

(percentage of children putting each scenario first)

Younger children are slightly more in favour of a world much the same as today than one which demonstrates increasing environmental concern. A considerable number also favour 'new technology'. As children get older, a future which is the same as today becomes increasingly unpopular. A third of 11 year old boys favour new technology and the proportion citing environmental concern has risen dramatically and corroborates our previous findings about the importance of this to children of 11.

The older children were also asked in which order they would *expect* the four scenarios to come about, i.e. as probable futures. It emerges that they do not have much faith in their preferred futures being realised: only 14% expect a future dominated by environmental concern. Just over a

Figure 4.2 Sam's future.

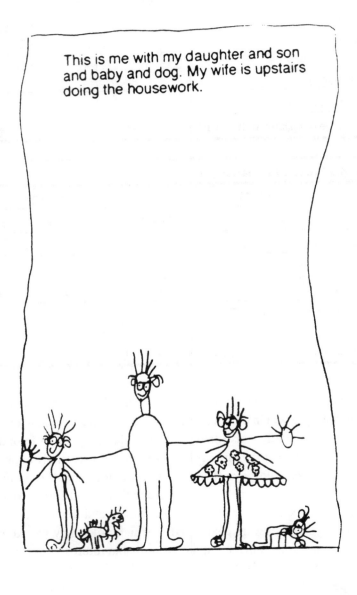

third think the world in the future will be the same as today, whilst a quarter expect either new technology or global disaster. Boys are slightly more pessimistic, being more likely to expect global warming and less likely to expect a world governed by environmental concern.

Visions of personal futures

Children were also asked to draw or write about the kind of future they would like if they could open a door into the world in 2020. The younger children's pictures mirror their responses to the four scenarios: the majority want life to be as it is now. Sam's picture is a classic example of this and of gender stereotyping at an early age!

For many 7 year old girls a 'rural paradise' scenario prevails. One girl's picture depicts 'lovely horses, goats, cows and sheep', and Hailey draws 'a beautiful world with a rainbow and a horse and a path and a gate and a sheep'. In none of these pictures is there any indication of twentieth century technology or any indication that it is the future, even though a quarter of the girls chose 'New technology' as their preferred scenario.

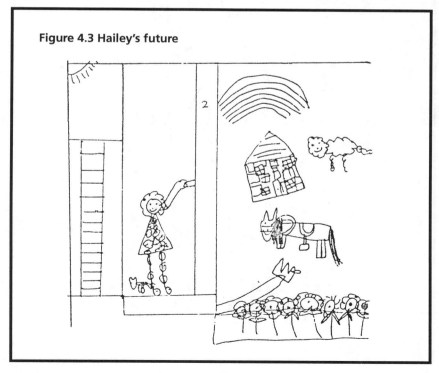

Figure 4.3 Hailey's future

Figure 4.4 Richard's future

I would like it if everybody & would be happy and joyful no violence and peace, their would be no (poor people) but people spending money on charities such as NSPCC and Oxfam or animals.

It would be nice for everyone to have a job and have a government who understand their country.

First it would be nice to have inventions which you don't use electric powers but have inventions which run by solar power.

I would like to see the numbers of animals increase and see no more sea pollution or oil spill out of sea. It would also be nice to see people not paying for practical things like beds in hospitals, and not having to put to much money in a bank to have a balance.

Some boys depict the future as a mythical past, a world of make-believe and excitement, endorsing the earlier findings that some 7 year olds find it hard to separate the real from the imaginary. One boy said he had drawn a pirate ship, with cannons, flag, pirates and a tree-house, because 'in the future there will be tree-houses and a warrior ship to play on'. Another boy's picture is of a cowboy with horse. 'In the future', he says, 'it's cowboy days and it would be good because everyone's going 'yee haa'.'

As we might expect, there are no such images in the 11 year olds' work. Instead images reflect the 'New technology' or 'Environmental concern' categories from the scenarios, often also showing a concern for social justice. Images relating to new technology are only drawn by boys. These often involve labour- saving devices, robots, high-tech toys and computers. It is interesting that when discussing poverty and unemployment, they make strong links between advanced technology and job losses but when asked to envision a world they would like, these concerns seem to disappear, subsumed by the attraction of new technology.

Figure 4.5 Charmaine's future

In the year 2020 I would like there to be
Trees, fields & grass,
And houses for the poor & lonely
For people to have jobs
No more war & fighting
I would like to live in a house with a big garden
And children who are sensible
With thoughts for the future
And happy minds.

Whilst some of the boys depict a purely 'high tech' world, Richard's comments are also typical and in many ways sum up the comments made by children when asked initially about their hopes and fears for the future. He is concerned about poverty, crime and pollution and wants a future where people have jobs and health care and where animals are protected.

For many 11 year old girls the issues are the same, but they are more likely to envisage themselves in a 'rural paradise', similar to the younger girls. Charmaine's is one such.

It seems that while some 11 year old boys favour a more technological society, the majority of all 11 year olds are concerned that social injustices should be alleviated and the environment protected. Seven year olds are beginning to endorse these values, but are also concerned that that future should be as it is today or as it was in a make-believe past.

Action and education

Although many 11 year olds do not feel it likely that their preferred future will come about, and both 7 and 11 year olds feel that world poverty and pollution will increase, there is still an optimism that, as individuals, they can make a difference. Nearly half of all primary pupils feel that they can do much to help the world become a better place and a further third that they can do a little. Two-thirds give examples of what they actually do, such as not dropping litter (62%), recycling (22%) and caring for others (20%). Although only a third of 11 year olds feel they have learnt a lot about global issues at school, over three quarters of all primary children think it is very important that they do learn about these issues.

7 year olds

Children of this age are aware of some of the national organisations working to improve social or global conditions, mentioning Barnados, a local hospice and Beavers (Cubs) because 'we planted some bulbs'. One boy feels his teacher's 'Greenteam' club has helped, as 'it plants things'. As well as planting and not dropping litter, they identify having positive attitudes as helping create a better future. One child has 'learnt how to be peaceful', and another claims that 'I help people. I don't be silly'. When asked what they have learnt in school about global issues, they are unable to give many examples, although one class has 'learnt about America' and another mentions the Arctic where 'in the olden days they caught fish out of a hole ....but now they've got oil'. In another school the children say they have done nothing yet but are emphatic that 'we'll do it in the bigger school'. All the children feel it is important that they do learn about these areas 'because you might be able to stop the bad things happening'.

11 year olds

Under 10% of 11 year olds are involved in organisations relating to global, social or economic issues: examples given are World Wide Fund for Nature, Oxfam, Friends of the Earth and animal welfare. Like the 7 year olds, many cite not dropping litter as something constructive they do, and many say their families recycle bottles and paper. Environmental action emerges for the first time: children mention 'not using CFCs' and cycling instead of getting their parents to use the car. Caring for others is seen as important: girls in particular mention 'being nice to each other' and 'not being prejudiced'.

The children maintain that their schools do not teach much about environmental or global issues, nor do they facilitate discussion about the future. Geographical studies of other localities are mentioned only once: a project on 'the rainforest and the Amazon'. At this school children also mention learning about other religions in RE, which they feel helps minimise prejudice. In another school children have learnt about solar power and electricity in science, but complain that any work about other countries is 'the ancient past'. They feel overwhelmingly that it is very important that they should learn 'more about the news', other countries, environmental issues, 'the greenhouse effect' and have 'more discussion classes'. Their justification is that it will help them 'to know what to do in the future'.

> Because when you get older you can look after it (the world) , and make sure you tell the next generation about it, because if you don't it won't be there for the next generation.

So, to summarise, by the end of primary school children are increasingly aware of social, economic and environmental issues and of the complexity of these issues. They are concerned about their own future and that of their local community and are fairly optimistic that the quality of life will improve for the majority. They are less optimistic about the global situation improving. Their choice of preferred futures indicates that many would like a future based on greater environmental awareness and their action as individuals reinforces this as an area of concern. Between the ages of 7 and 11 children's ideas about the environment and global issues develop a great deal but this is not generally a result of the taught curriculum. Pupils indicate that they have had little teaching in this area and would welcome more. They wish to be better informed about the world around them and better able to contribute to its future.

Chapter 5

Secondary school pupils

In 2020 I imagine that people will be more aware of the environment and the consequences of burning fossil fuels. There will be more alternative sources of energy such as solar, biomass, geothermal and nuclear. I can see the world becoming a better place but only when attitudes have changed and we aren't so concerned with our own personal needs. However, I fear this will only come about after a major disaster. — Boy, age 18.

Personal futures

Interest in their personal future is high for children of secondary school age. More than two-thirds of pupils aged 14 say they often think about this. The percentage of boys and girls thinking about their future is the same but girls are twice as likely to talk about it with friends. For pupils aged 18 interest is even higher, with 82% often thinking about their personal future. Over half say they talk about it often with friends and, again, girls are more likely to do so than boys.

Secondary school pupils are very aware of the need to do well at school to obtain a good job if they are to achieve the 'good life', ie material success. Their hopes and fears centre around preparation for adult life, with relationships (family and partners) also being important.

14 year olds

One of the main concerns of 14 year olds is getting a good job, but only a fifth of boys mention its prerequisite, a good education, as one of their hopes. It may be that they assume its importance and merely mention the end product. Happiness emerges as a hope in its own right, ie not linked to material success, as it was for the primary school children.

> I want to live a long and happy life. I want to stay in contact with my friends after school and college.

Boys of this age also prioritise the good life and material success. Both boys and girls attach greater importance to good relationships than do older secondary pupils, but it is particularly important to the girls. Many mention families and partners.

The fears of 14 year olds focus on the same areas, but with different emphases. More than half the girls are worried about something happening to their families, and just under half worry about having no job or ill health. Personal violence (attacks, rape) is also mentioned by a third of the girls but very few boys.

> I fear unhappiness. Death of my family. War.

> Not having my mum and dad there when I need them.

Table 5.1 Personal hopes for future (ages 14 and 18)					
	Age 14		Age 18		Secondary
	girls	boys	girls	boys	Total
Employment	88	82	75	73	79
Good life	35	59	33	61	47
Relationships	68	49	28	39	46
Education	48	20	72	36	44
Happiness	25	10	53	42	33
Health	10	33	14	24	20
(percentage of pupils mentioning these hopes)					
Note: Because pupils could mention as many hopes or fears as they wished, the numbers in tables 5.1-6 add up to more than 100%.					

14 year old boys, however, are concerned about ill health and dying young, and give cancer and AIDs as examples. Just under half cite no money and unemployment as a fear and over a third worry about being homeless.

18 year olds.

These pupils have nearly completed their schooling and are on the brink of adult life. Their two priorities appear to be a good job and a good education, although twice as many girls as boys mention the latter. Relationships are not as important for 18 year old girls as they were for the 14 year olds, but many more cite happiness as a hope. Boys still want the good life and a good job, and again slightly more boys than girls are concerned about good health. An 18 year old girl writes:

> I hope that I obtain the career that I wish to have. That I remain healthy and live for a long time. That I settle down with someone when I wish to.

Two-thirds of boys and girls worry about being unemployed or having an unsatisfying job and just under half are concerned about the possibilities of having no money and ill-health. A third fear an adult world where they have no friends and a similar number are concerned about something happening to their families. The fear of the younger pupils about home-lessness seems to have disappeared and is only mentioned by a few boys. Many of this age group mention happiness and personal fulfilment as a

Table 5.2 Personal fears for future (ages 14 and 18)					
	Age 14		Age 18		Secondary
	girls	boys	girls	bpys	Total
Unemployment	49	43	61	58	53
Health problems	41	57	42	42	46
Family problems	54	25	31	24	34
No money	15	43	33	39	33
Homelessness	21	35	8	12	19
(percentage of pupils mentioning these fears)					

hope, and we now see the converse of this as pupils cite a the fear of 'doing nothing with my life' or being 'dead inside' as an indicator of an unfulfilled life. Many sum up their fears movingly:

I fear being alone in the horribly adult society that currently exists.

I fear lack of confidence. Not feeling happy or self-fulfilled.

To have no friends. To have no money. To die.

Despite the desire for material success and a good education, it is apparent that for school leavers there is an understanding that these things do not bring happiness in themselves. Their comments reveal an awareness of the emotional complexities of adult life and of the difficulties they feel they may encounter in establishing themselves in secure relationships and with friends.

Local futures

The majority of secondary school students claim to be uninterested in the future of their local area. Over two-thirds say they think about it only sometimes, and a third of boys say they never think about it. They talk about it even less: half the girls say that they sometimes discuss it with friends but only one third of boys do. Like the primary school children, it appears that they do not watch regional news on TV nor read local newspapers much.

This apparent disinterest is not evident, however, when they describe their hopes and fears for their local area. Their comments indicate a common concern for the built and natural environment, for an end to crime and violence and for improved social and economic conditions. In reality, their concern for the local area is high.

14 year olds

This age group expresses a very real desire for better local amenities. They want more shops and improved leisure facilities for adults and children. Two girls want a future with:

Not so much crime. More things to do. More shops.

A clean area for my children to play in. A nice place where my children can go outside and be safe.

Table 5.3 Hopes for local area (ages 14 and 18)					
	Age 14		Age 18		Secondary
	girls	boys	girls	boys	Total
Better amenities	59	43	38	38	45
Less crime	37	35	49	44	41
Less pollution	35	57	16	25	33
Prosperity	12	10	51	59	33
Environmental concern	39	27	35	25	32
(percentage of pupils mentioning these hopes)					

Along with improved amenities is a hope for increased environmental awareness — that people will want to protect the countryside and that their area 'becomes an environmentally friendly place'. Writing about fears for their local area, crime emerges as a serious concern: more than half are worried that it may increase. A new concern also emerges among these older pupils — that their local area may grow too large and become spoiled in the process. This is a fear expressed by a third of 14 year olds. One boy worries that his small town 'will be made into a city', whilst another hopes it will 'stay the same way it is now'. For some, tourists are seen as a threat:

I fear that there will be too many tourists who leave lots of litter.

The responses of the children to questions about specific issues reveal that they are not optimistic about social and economic conditions becoming better in the future. Asked about poverty, violence, unemployment and pollution, pupils think that things will get worse. It is only in relation to attitudes, specifically with reference to race and gender, that they think there will be an improvement.

Discussions with these pupils indicate that unemployment and poverty are linked in their minds. Over a third think both will get worse, the same percentage think things will be the same and only a quarter hold out hope for improved conditions. Their arguments consistently centre on two areas. Firstly there is the belief, found repeatedly, that technology is causing unemployment:

Table 5.4 Fears for local area (ages 14 and 18)					
	Age 14		Age 18		Secondary
	girls	boys	girls	boys	Total
More crime	57	54	63	61	59
Unemployment	29	21	57	48	39
More pollution	43	54	23	29	37
Worsening environment	37	23	34	23	29
Increased size	33	23	20	23	25
(percentage of pupils mentioning these fears)					

There will be more (unemployment) because machines at the moment are taking over jobs. As technology progresses there'll be more people out of work.

It's to do with modernisation and industry... It's all done by computers.

Secondly there is a conviction that over-population in their local area and in Britain is a major cause of unemployment and poverty. Whereas one girl maintains that 'there will be more poverty because there will be more people', others try to give reasons for this.

There are always people from other countries coming over getting jobs and people in our country aren't getting the jobs they would have done.

There are more people because less and less people are dying because the medical conditions are getting better.

Other pupils maintain that it is 'the recession' which is the cause of poverty and the fault of 'the government' and one boy insists that some people 'are purposely unemployed to cheat the system'. The hopes of pupils who feel things might improve centre mainly on the creation of more jobs through technology. One boy is ambivalent. He thinks poverty will be reduced but at a cost:

If there was a nuclear war that would reduce the population and so there would be more jobs.

For some pupils of this age there is a clear link between poverty and violence. One comments that:

Everyone's getting sacked and the bosses are getting pay rises... there's two distinct classes..so civil war might break out.

Somewhat less dramatically, others relate unemployment to crime and fear a rise in both. Only one in ten think violence will decrease in the future. Of those who think it will stay the same, one says that there are 'bound to be more weapons' but that 'the police will have better ways of controlling criminals so it will balance out'. For many, rising crime is associated with inadequate policing, and pupils living in isolated villages give examples of the time taken for the police to respond to incidents. City pupils have an awareness of 'no go' areas, 'places you don't go at night and the weekend' but even so insist that their areas are 'not as bad as other places'.

Some areas are worse. People get attacked in their cars..at traffic lights.

You see it on TV... Crime's going up, the suicide rate's going up.

There is a tendency to blame television for the increase in violence, and there is concern that 'small kids' are particularly influenced. One boy cites the recent murder of a toddler by children as an example of young boys who 'were definitely influenced by violence (on TV)' and another explains:

Children get confused ...like fact and fiction. They don't know the difference. They see someone get hit and then they get up and children feel they can do it... young children ...7 or 8.

These boys do not see themselves as being adversely influenced, but are concerned about the impact on children younger than themselves.

Pollution is another key issue over which a majority of 14 year olds are pessimistic. They blame 'cars and exhaust pipes' and emissions from factories. Whilst they show an appreciation that things are improving in some areas (only 'a few aerosols have CFCs' now, and 'people do use the park and ride') there is also an awareness that it is an issue that requires efforts that not all people want to make.

Some people want to do a lot about the environment but other companies think it doesn't matter and that it'll get cleaned up by someone else.

The pupils who are optimistic cite evidence of increased awareness which they feel will influence people to care more. One girl says there is 'a lot about it in magazines' and a boy is convinced things will improve when there are 'laws to cut down pollution'. He also has faith in technology to find 'new ways to clean up the atmosphere'. There is a realisation here that the forces influencing any issue are complex and so are the possible solutions.

In the area of prejudice and racist attitudes there is more optimism. Whilst over half think things will be the same, a third feel there will be an improvement. One child feels attitudes must improve:

If the world's to progress then you have to get on with other races.

Other children feel that 'people are mixing together more and becoming friends' and that relationships will continue to be improve because:

More people are being taught about it... Now there isn't half as much as there used to be. People were brought up to be prejudiced, but its getting better. We're all human beings.

There are some reservations. The police are felt to be racist and so are 'some films'. London is seen as a racist area, unlike their home towns. Conditions are seen as 'worse elsewhere', with a fear that the 'elsewhere' may become their town tomorrow.

18 year olds

These young adults in their final year of school share many of the concerns of the 14 year olds. They too hope that their local area will be less polluted but they put more emphasis on increased environmental awareness as a solution. They hope that this increased awareness will result in the countryside being protected. Just under half hope that there will be less crime and a slightly smaller percentage mention better amenities (shops and leisure facilities). What they see as most important to the local community is greater prosperity. This, they feel, would alleviate poverty, provide jobs and stem urban decline. Their fears mirror their hopes: rises in crime, unemployment, a worsening environment and urban deterioration. One pupil fears that 'the local school will close; the bus route will stop', while another worries 'that the countryside [will] become the home of humans rather than animals'. A girl writes:

> I fear it becoming too big... it keeps developing, ie housing estates on the outskirts,... the crime rate increasing ie vandalism, burglaries, which worries me...

Speaking about specific issues, 18 year olds are not optimistic that the future will be better in their local area. Two-thirds feel violence will be worse, and nearly a half think unemployment will be worse. Greater political awareness, however, can now be seen emerging. One group of pupils debate the impact of voting Labour or Conservative on the alleviation of poverty and then discuss whether people are in fact poorer now or whether this 'depends on the definition'. Whilst most think poverty will increase, one pupils argues that:

> Poor people are more susceptible to disease and illness... They are more likely to take illegal drugs, so they are more likely to die...

There is optimism that people's attitudes towards both racial prejudice and sex role stereotyping will improve. Pupils feel that it takes a long time for attitudes to change, possibly over generations, but that this is happening slowly and will continue to do so. Issues relating to equality are more talked about now and there is more awareness among both men and women. They feel that gender 'is more in the employers' consciousness than it was in the past' and that there will be less racial prejudice, because 'people are more accepting than they used to be'. Eighteen year olds are the most optimistic group about this issue.

Global futures

More than half of all the secondary school children claim to think about the future of the world often or very often and most thought about it sometimes. Three quarters often see programmes on television relating to the world's future, and half read about related issues. Interest in world issues seems to be much higher than for local area issues, although the disinterest initially claimed about local issues was not matched by what was subsequently said.

Table 5.5 Hopes for global future (ages 14 and 18)					
	Age 14		Age 18		Secondary
	girls	boys	girls	boys	Total
Absence of war	75	82	87	73	79
Less pollution	40	63	41	33	44
Food/no poverty	38	35	38	39	38
Good relationships	35	10	46	33	38
Environmental awareness	10	14	51	36	28
(percentage of pupils mentioning these hopes)					

The greatest hope is for the absence of war or, as one 18 year old girl puts it, 'for war to become peace'. Good relationships between countries are seen as one way of ensuring this, hence the hope that countries will negotiate and be on good terms with each other. Although pollution is still a key concern, a broader perspective emerges of environmental awareness, with an emphasis on attitudes and action. A boy of 14, for example, wants 'more solar and green power' and an 18 year old girl hopes for 'global peace, eradication of poverty and global greening'. Over a third of secondary pupils nominate the alleviation of starvation and poverty as one of their hopes, particularly in third world countries. Girls appear to put more emphasis on good relationships between countries and it is the older pupils, again particularly girls, who hope for increased environmental awareness.

14 year olds

The fears of this age group for the global future show them sharing fear of war with the older and younger pupils. However, no children of primary age mention nuclear war whereas, a quarter of 14 year olds do so. One boy thinks nuclear war may occur 'if we run out of resources', whilst for another:

There may be nuclear war if all the countries disagree. There's just one button... they could blow up England with one button... That's quite scary.

There is no clear indication of who might be the instigators of such a war, only a notion that war might just 'come about'. Pupils think that war can be the result of 'more poverty in other countries', as well as resource depletion. Nearly two-thirds of these pupils expect the world to be a more violent place in the future.

When asked about the possibilities for world poverty being alleviated in the future, very few pupils think the situation will improve. Most think that poverty and unemployment will continue to rise, or at best stay the same. Again technology is cited as a reason for increased unemployment and subsequent poverty. This is at odds with the examples given of poverty and technology in relation to specific countries. India, seen as having no technology, is said to be a poor country where things are unlikely to improve in the future. However another pupil acknowledges that 'in France and America they're further ahead in technology than us' but asserts that they are not poor countries as a result. Pupils of this age appear to be aware of social and economic conditions on a global scale but to have a rather hazy understanding of the causes. They appear to stereotype countries into 'poor' or 'high tech' but show little understanding of the variations which may exist within one country or even on a whole continent. Whereas they suggest many solutions at a local level for the alleviation of homelessness and poverty, pupils find it harder to do on a global scale.

Table 5.6 Fears for global future (ages 14 and 18)

	Age 14		Age 18		Secondary
	girls	boys	girls	boys	Total
War	57	69	73	69	67
Pollution	49	43	41	47	45
Poverty/no food	27	26	32	28	28
Global warming	32	29	27	13	25
(percentage of pupils mentioning these fears)					

Fourteen year olds are equally pessimistic about pollution being reduced in the future. This is seen as due to 'bigger industries', more traffic and more factories 'chucking stuff in the sea'. Oil spillages are also mentioned. Again we see pupils trying to sort out the advantages and disadvantages of increased technology. Africa is deemed a continent with little pollution because 'they haven't got much cars', whereas Japan has 'a lot of pollution because everything's such high technology'. One pupil is convinced that attitude plays a part:

> I'd have thought poorer countries, they want to recycle, because they can't afford to make things. They're not doing much to pollute the atmosphere, but rich countries, they think 'what the heck', they can't be bothered to recycle... like acid rain; it doesn't affect us. We make it and it just goes up to Norway.

Linked with pollution is an awareness of the dangers of global warming and the depletion of the ozone layer, and over a quarter name it as one of their fears.

> My fears are for the hole in the ozone layer to get bigger. For there to be a massive world war. For wildlife to disappear.

The consensus of 14 year olds is that life will not improve for most people on the planet in the future. They see living conditions as worsening and are very concerned about a deteriorating environment. However there is optimism about increased awareness in other areas. Pupils think that the understanding they now have of prejudice and stereotyping means there will be less racism in the future and greater gender equality. They also believe people that are more aware of health issues and that as a result people will adopt healthier lifestyles. In spite of their obvious interest in global affairs, the children appear less well informed than about local issues.

18 year olds

The hopes of these young adults centre on the absence of war, together with good relationships with other countries and a better environment. This includes less pollution as well as increased environmental awareness.

I want humans to become part of nature, not nature's controller. I want it to be habitable until the sun blows up, not until the air becomes too toxic to breathe.

When asked to describe their fears, war again emerges as a fear. One third mention nuclear war. Starvation and poverty are a concern and one girl fears...

That children will grow up in a world full of poverty and hatred.

Global pollution is a concern for nearly half of this age group and many mention global warming, the depletion of the ozone layer and deforestation.

I fear the destruction of the rain forests, expansion of human populations into all natural areas, and global warming...

Two-thirds of 18 year olds think pollution will be worse in the future and recognise that averting this is not a simple issue. One group argues that it is only the easy things that are being tackled, not the underlying causes of pollution, and there is general agreement that not enough is being done to encourage recycling.

Two-thirds are pessimistic about poverty or unemployment being alleviated on a global scale. However, these pupils are less likely to be satisfied with generalised statements and to question and acknowledge the complexities of the issues. One 18 year old boy thinks there will be more poverty in the third word because 'there's not much contraception' but others put forward different ideas:

There will be more poverty... a bigger gap between North and South and between developing and non-developing countries.

I disagree — I think the Northern countries will realise the Southern countries need help.

The pupils debate the influence of different governments and mention class for the first time. For one pupil, the future will bring an even more 'exploited working class' and many feel that the gap between rich and poor will get worse. Again technology is seen as a culprit in the creation of unemployment, but it is now linked with power:

Technology will go too far. Everyone who has power will become too greedy, people with no power will be at their mercy.

Whereas the oldest pupils are the least optimistic about economic and environmental conditions improving, they are the most optimistic about greater equality coming through a change in attitudes. They feel there will be less racial prejudice and, with reference to the position of women, three-quarters think women throughout the world will have greater equality. One girl explains that:

Women have (had) the qualifications but a lot of people giving them the jobs have been men, but now women are in those positions its going to be easier... Everyone is more aware of that.

Some boys are not so quick to concede that women might do any kind of work:

There will always be a place for men doing dirty jobs and women doing other jobs. The physical differences will always mean they do different jobs. Men are stronger than women...

These young adults are equally divided about whether life for people throughout the world will be the same or worse. Only 20% think it will be better. They are less optimistic than younger children about this and less optimistic for the future of the world than they are for the future of their local area.

Visions of the future

Choice of scenarios

Secondary school pupils were given the same four scenarios to consider: Same as today, New technology, Environmental concern and Global disaster (see Table 4.7).

They were asked first to rank the scenarios in the order they would most like them to come about.

Nearly two-thirds of secondary school children prefer the environmental concern scenario. This increases with age and is especially prevalent among girls. Boys not attracted by this option are most likely to favour a world with new technology, although this appears to decrease as a preference as pupils get older. A small proportion of 14 year olds wish life to be as it is today none of the older pupils do.

When asked in which order they *expect* these scenarios to come about, the picture is different. Eighteen year olds are the least optimistic. Hardly any expect a world based on environmental concern, whereas one fifth of 14 year olds hold out hope that it will be. A small proportion of all secondary pupils fear that global disaster will occur, but most expect the world to be as it is today or to be dominated by new technology.

Visions of personal futures

The pupils were also asked to envisage the kind of world they would like in 2020. Their visions indicate a belief that new technology may help create a better world with better social and economic conditions.

> Technology has advanced incredibly and life is a mass of computers and automatic everything, but the simple joys of taking a walk in the park, walking along the sea front or going for a hike in the lake district are still not lost. The earth is luscious and green... Poor countries will be a thing of the past with all people sharing wealth and technology. (Boy, 14)

The eradication of poverty, homelessness and inequality features in many of the visions. Another boy of 14 writes:

> At night there will be no beggars or homeless on the streets. Unemployment will be gone. Drug abuse is lower than ever as the poor who wish to be rid of their troubles will not need them.

Table 5.7 Preferred scenarios (ages 14 and 18)					
	Age 14		Age 18		Secondary
	girls	boys	girls	boys	Total
Environmental concern	60	49	77	54	60
New technology	33	47	22	42	36
Same as today	10	12	0	0	6
Global disaster	0	3	0	2	1
(percentage of pupils putting each scenario first)					

One girl of 13 sees a future which does not encompass new technology but focuses on the alleviation of poverty, against a 'rural paradise' backdrop. She also focuses on attitudes and social conditions:

I can walk down a road where there is very little traffic. There is a huge park with lots of grass, flowers and a safe play area... There are lots of rain forests and no poverty. You can walk past the job centre on a Monday morning and it is empty except for the people working there. You switch on the TV and you hear good news and achievements, not war and hunger. There are no perfect images of models and people are happy with themselves, and do not need to have plastic surgery. There is less anorexia in teenagers and unwanted pregnancies.

The issues appear to be the same for older pupils but they show greater awareness of the ways in which a better world might come about and of the barriers to change. Many mention increased political activity and alternative sources of energy. An 18 year old girl sees a world where 'pollution will not be a problem, the energy we need will come from the sun'. Some are doubtful about the possibilities for change. One says it would be easy to say 'less pollution and greater equality, but I don't really think it'll be like that'. Another cannot envisage a better future:

I think the divide between rich and poor will be greater. There will still be war and a nuclear war threat. It's human nature to say 'not in my backyard' or 'it's somebody else's problem', so not much will change.

Table 5.8 Expected scenarios (ages 14 and 18)				
	Age 14		Age 18		Secondary
	girls	boys	girls	boys	Total
New technology	47	43	38	45	43
Same as today	26	33	43	45	37
Environmental concern	16	22	3	3	11
Global disaster	12	8	16	6	11
(percentage of pupils putting each scenario first)					

Finally, one 18 year old boy manages to combine his visions of better social conditions with a world of fun and positive attitudes:

> There's music everywhere...there'll be Snakebite on the radio and kids jumping in the streets kicking footballs.... No cars except long beautiful old Citroens and Fords and there'll be no litter and people won't want or need to steal and everyone'll be high on life and making it. People will *want* to go to school because they *want* to learn and they'll all read all the time and get as excited about books and records as they do about Segas. There'll be bands practising in every possible space — in backrooms and garages — and people will respect each other and *like* each other. Maybe they'll even give a -----. Who knows?

Action and education

Despite having clear visions of the kind of world they would like, secondary school pupils are ambivalent about whether they can play any part in this process. Half the 14 year olds feel they can do a little to make the world a better place, while 40% think they can do a good deal. The older secondary pupils are less optimistic: a third feel they can do much but two thirds feel they can only do a little. Some mention belonging to organisations acting for change (Amnesty, Greenpeace) but most examples centre on individual action. Of the two-thirds who claim that they do something now to help make the world a better place, just over half mention recycling, a third buy products because they are environmentally friendly and a quarter say they do not drop litter. Schools do not appear to teach much about global issues — only a quarter of pupils say they have learnt much about this at school.

14 year olds

Pupils of this age are aware of many organisations working for change and vary widely in their support for them. Some pupils give examples of supporting charities:

> I do the 24 hour famine every year and I do things for a charity about bears... You write to countries which have dancing bears.

One boy names three organisations (World Wide Fund for Nature, Greenpeace, Oxfam) but says he's 'never known of anyone who belonged to one'. Another student adds that 'they don't advertise very well' and so are not appealing to people of their age. He feels such organisations should be active 'in a fun way... not boring meetings'.

The importance of the media in reaching young people and affecting attitudes is reiterated in the discussion over environmental action. They agree that recycling is becoming more prevalent but that it needs to be given a higher media profile.

> There should be more recycling. It should be more promoted — more advertisements on TV, saying 'do it now before it's too late'.

Girls are twice as likely as boys to buy products because they are environmentally friendly. Examples given are deodorants without CFCs and products not tested on animals. Girls are also more likely to suggest sharing ideas and challenging prejudices as a way of bringing about a better future. One girl explains how she has changed her mother's attitudes:

> My mum used to be slightly racist because she was brought up in a racist community but now she's not racist one bit because I talked to her and explained everything to her.

Most of the pupils feel they have only learnt a little about global issues at school. Examples are given of lessons on pollution, global warming, the earth's resources and natural disasters in other countries. In all cases the pupils conclude that they are not taught enough, and that they need more knowledge to enable them as adults to 'do something about things'. Schools attempt to foster caring attitudes through charity work and one girl praises her school for its work for the Save the Children Fund. They raise a lot of money and there are 'lots of leaflets in the library'. The students cannot recall any discussion on their personal or the global future, other than a little careers advice. 'We don't get the chance to go deeply into things' says one girl, and another adds 'I don't really know what to expect in the future at all'.

18 year olds

These pupils are sceptical about their ability to bring about change. A boy comments that he does not think 'there's very much any individual can do', and another concedes that change is possible 'but everybody would have to believe in it'. Boys appear more pessimistic and are more likely to offer political solutions than girls. One boy says that the best thing he could do to make the world better:

> would be to join the socialist party of GB... be a typical lefty student! Because if not... the world will be quickly uninhabitable if we carry on.

Girls, in contrast, are often advocates of charities working for change. One is a member of Amnesty and writes letter to political prisoners; another is about to do voluntary work with disabled people or AIDS sufferers. These girls argue that there is something they as individuals can do, since 'if everyone takes action, you're not an individual'. Boys and girls agree that for change to be effective it has to be 'on a range of levels' — personal, local and global.

At the end of their formal education the pupils say they have covered personal issues (drugs, careers) to some extent, but have only touched on global issues, in geography or biology. One boy sees this as the fault of the National Curriculum which is too restrictive. Another says:

> the problem with schools these days is they're not allowed to talk about politics. Teachers have to be neutral.

The majority of the students feel that have not been taught enough about global issues or issues related to their own future as adult citizens.

Thus, to summarise, by the end of secondary school young people are concerned about their personal future but are fairly optimistic about achieving material success and finding personal happiness. They are far less optimistic about the quality of life improving in their local community or globally, however, believing that poverty, unemployment and pollution will increase. Although they are increasingly aware of the complexity of these issues, they have learnt little about them at school and do not feel adequately prepared for their impending role as global citizens. They have visions of the future they would like but little idea of how these might be made real.

Chapter 6

Overview and implications

In 2020 the world will be cleaner and brighter. At night there will be no beggars or homeless on the streets. Unemployment miraculously will be gone. People will be healthier and more friendly than in 1994. Crime will be at an all-time low and there will be less threat of war to the world. There will be racial equality for all. The space programme will have improved greatly and the ships will be a bit like the Enterprise from Star Trek. Pollution will be non-existent. Drug abuse will be lower than ever as the poor who wish to be rid of their troubles will not need them. — Boy, age 14.

Age differences

Previous research into children's views of the future has focused on primary or secondary pupils but none has specifically compared the findings at different stages of a child's development. The research discussed here thus adds significantly to our understanding, allowing us to see how children's views differ according to age, and giving an insight into how the optimism of the 7 year old is transformed into the pessimism of the school leaver. There are many implications for schools arising from these findings.

7 year olds

The 7 year olds in our survey were only in their second year of compulsory schooling, at an age where many would argue that the curriculum should be confined to their immediate geographical surroundings and immediate family. Indeed, before the advent of the National Curriculum many children of this age were taught very little geography or history, in the belief that they were too young to understand concepts of time or place (HMI, 1989). The research reported in Chapter 4 belies this notion.

Children of this age are concerned not only about their personal future but also about the future of their local community and the global future. Although some 7 year olds find it difficult to imagine themselves as adults, for the majority it is something they are concerned about and wish for reassurance on. That reality and fantasy sit side by side in their visions of the future is not a reason for ignoring their interest. Children are trying to make sense of the world and their role in it and the teacher should be facilitating this process. These children are already aware that a job is important to their future well-being and they hope for a degree of material success; but fears lurk that not only may there be family problems, no jobs and ill-health in the future, but that there may also be monsters, dinosaurs and burglars to contend with.

The 7 year olds' concern about their local area is based on a mixture of the actual evidence around them and ideas from the media. They are aware of social conditions — unemployment and homelessness — and at the same time fear that wars seen on television may materialise in their own area. Some children are beginning to link cause and effect e.g. poverty and unemployment. Although there is uncertainty about what the future may hold, there is confidence that things will get better.

7 year olds are interested in the future of the world, however hazy their world map may be. Their understanding of global issues is evidence of a stage in children's development when they are trying to sort out the real world from the imaginary or the world presented by the media. Some children are able to name countries and give examples of global poverty and pollution, but a few of them still see the world as potentially peopled by aliens, or in danger of exploding. Although 7 year olds are optimistic that life for people all over the world will get better, they are ambivalent about whether poverty or pollution will be alleviated. They are the most optimistic of all age groups, feeling that life will be better for themselves

and for others. They are keen to participate in this process and to learn more at school about the future and global issues. Their understanding about helping create a better future is at a very practical and basic level: they don't drop litter and they are 'good children'. When asked what kind of future they would like, nearly half want it to be the same as it is now. Again this illustrates the stability they would like in the future. They want the security of family and friends, set in a rural environment. This is perhaps not surprising in children who are just becoming aware of the dangers of the world around them, and of the challenges of the adult world.

Although many want a world the same as today, one third would like a world characterised by environmental concern. This indicates that environmental awareness is developing in children at a very young age. Many of their individual visions of the future are stereotyped: they depict themselves as mothers with 'long hair' and lots of children, or as fathers in a conventional role (cf Figure 4.2). The primary teacher clearly has a complex task. She needs to alert children to the possibilities of the future, to allay their fears and build on their hopes, but at the same time she needs to challenge gender stereotyping if the prejudices of previous generations are not to be reproduced.

11 year olds

Eleven year olds at primary school have more in common with 14 and 18 year olds than with 7 year olds. The fantasy world of monsters and dragons has disappeared, and their hopes and fears bear more resemblance to those of the older children. Like the 7 year olds they hope for a good job and material well-being, but in common with the secondary pupils they also want a good education. Their fears have changed dramatically. They now fear personal violence e.g. rape, mugging and the addiction of cigarettes and drugs. Consideration of these fears needs to be an essential part of personal and social education in the primary school.

Eleven year olds' awareness of and interest in local affairs is also more sophisticated than that of 7 year olds. They are keen to see their local area improved; in particular they want less pollution, more recycling and less traffic. They care about facilities for the homeless, for the disabled and for children but say there is little discussion of these issues at school. Although they are now able to distinguish between the world of make-believe and the real world, some in common with 7 year olds, have not yet managed to disentangle world affairs from local affairs. Many still fear that the violence they have witnessed on television (war in Bosnia or terrorism) may affect their town.

The concerns of 11 year olds about global issues also have more in common with secondary pupils than with the younger children. They are concerned about increasing pollution and poverty and hope for an end to war and violence. War is hardly mentioned by 7 year olds but is a major concern for three-quarters of 11 year olds as they become more aware of what is happening in the wider world.

These children are beginning to realise that many issues are not straightforward and that certain actions may have undesirable consequences. They appreciate that new technology may offer solutions but that it may also bring more problems, eg unemployment. Their preferred futures show that they are very keen to have a world based on environmental concern and they show a commitment to this by not dropping litter, by recycling or by buying environmentally friendly products — something new to this age group and not found amongst the 7 year olds. Commitment to improving the environment and to learning about global issues seems highest at this age. Although they are less optimistic than the younger children that social conditions will improve, they nevertheless hold a naive belief that everyone *is* concerned about improving the planet and they would like to be a part of this.

14 year olds

It is at this age that pupils begin to lose their conviction that everyone is working for a better environment in the future. Along with an awareness of the complexities of the issues is a realisation that not everyone feels that it is important to get rid of pollution, for example, They acknowledge that certain people do not care about polluting the environment and that new technology is not necessarily an answer to many problems.

This increased sophistication is mirrored in their personal hopes, where we see for the first time, a desire expressed for happiness *per se*. They show understanding that happiness and material well-being are not necessarily synonymous and that the former may be more important. Unemployment and ill health are still concerns. Fewer in this age group are worried about personal violence — it has transferred into a fear about crime in general in their local area. They are also concerned that their local area may be spoilt by growing too large or becoming run down, a fear not found among primary children. Pupils of this age are looking for reasons for the situation they see around them. New technology and immigration are blamed for increasing unemployment and television is blamed for increasing crime. Some pupils realise that there are many causes and that the issues are complex; others think there are simple and obvious solutions.

The eradication of global poverty and pollution are key concerns for the 14 year olds as they were for the 11 year olds. However, their thinking has now developed to include an awareness of global warming and depletion of the ozone layer. Some mention the dangers of deforestation. Whereas war is still a major concern, a quarter of all 14 year olds now refer specifically to nuclear war. It is unclear where this fear has come from. Since none of the pupils mention learning about it in school, it is presumably from the media. They are less optimistic than 11 year olds about world conditions improving and are ambivalent about whether they can do anything themselves to help make the world a better place.

Fourteen year olds have done some work on global issues in science and geography lessons and have covered some areas relating to their personal futures (sex education and careers) in personal, social and moral education. In all cases, however, pupils say that this has not been enough. They wish to know more and to be better informed so that they may take action, now and in the future. There is evidence that some schools are good at raising awareness of the work done by charities, but not that this has been extended to any in-depth examination of the causes of poverty and social injustice. There is little evidence of curriculum time which examines social change and yet pupils are questioning current socio-economic conditions and hoping for a future where there will be greater justice and equality. However, it may be that teachers have attempted to cover these issues but that pupils have not fully understood.

18 year olds

As these pupils are on the brink of adulthood, it is perhaps not surprising that they are more interested in their personal future than any other age group. Like the 14 year olds, they hope for material success, a good education and employment, but they are now twice as likely to mention happiness as a goal in its own right and put less emphasis on good relationships (family, partner). Lack of a job is their chief fear, followed by health and money problems. They are still positive, however, that their life will be better in the future than it is now.

This optimism does not extend to the local community. Eighteen year olds are the least positive about conditions improving either locally or globally. Whilst they hope that there will be increased prosperity in their local area, they also fear more crime and unemployment. Unemployment worries twice as many 18 as 14 year olds. The exception to their pessimism is in relation to attitude changes, about which they are the most optimistic of all age groups. Despite their fear of greater poverty and unemployment, they feel strongly that there will be less racism and greater gender equality in the future. They are even more convinced of this than 14 or 11 year olds.

Their understanding of environmental issues is now more complex and they are four times more likely than the 14 year olds to mention greater environmental awareness as a hope. They have a greater understanding of the concerns mentioned first by 14 year olds (global warming, destruction of the ozone layer) and an awareness that there are varying degrees of support for environmental improvement. While 18 year olds, more than any age group, want a future based on environmental concern, they are the least convinced that this will come about. They do not want a future the same as today but fear that this, or a future based on new technology, is what will materialise. This is perhaps the root of the pessimism of the 18 year olds: they now have a clear idea of what they would like but no faith that the future will bring change for the better.

Although some 18 year olds give examples of action they take to effect change, many are sceptical of the influence they can have. They are aware of a system 'out there' which influences people's lives but do not see themselves as part of that process. Awareness of the political dimension first appears among this age group. They are beginning to understand that people with power and political influence can create and alleviate current socio- economic conditions but, again, they feel they have little access to such power. Their awareness has not come from school; no mention is made of citizenship or political education. Like the 14 year olds, they have touched on global issues in science and geography and have covered sex, drugs and careers in personal education, but they have not discussed politics or their future role as active citizens with the ability to bring about change. All maintain that they have not had sufficient education about either global issues or their own future.

Gender differences

Whether a school is in a rural or urban area and whether children come from a relatively affluent or deprived backgrounds does not appear to influence their hopes and fears for the future. The only variable, other than age, which significantly influences their responses is gender. From the age of 7 through to 18, gender is a key factor in determining how children think and feel about the future.

Girls of all ages express more interest than boys in their own future, the future of their community and the world. Far more girls than boys (especially of secondary school age) think it is important to study these issues at school. With the exception of 18 year old girls, they are much more likely to hope for good relationships (partners, children) in the future, and less likely to mention the good life and material success, which are mentioned by twice as many boys. The importance of good relationships to girls is extended to relationships between countries, which they also mention far more often. A good education is also seen as more important by girls than boys, as is happiness *per se*. For both a good job is important, but older boys worry more about possible ill-health and homelessness.

Regarding whether they feel they can make a difference themselves, twice as many secondary school girls as boys feel they can do something. Half the girls feel they can do 'a lot', compared to a third of boys. Boys of 18 are the most cynical or disillusioned: only 16% feel they can do much. Boys of this age are more likely than girls to mention the possibility of political action but do not themselves engage with it. Of those who give examples of what they can do, boys are more keen on environmental action (recycling, cycling), while more girls mention buying environmentally friendly products. Girls also mention the importance of influencing people through sharing ideas.

There is less variance over their hopes and fears for the local community. Boys show slightly more concern than girls about pollution but otherwise they are remarkably similar, focusing on improved amenities, less crime and greater prosperity. Boys of 11 and 14 are more concerned than girls of the same age about local traffic and want cycle tracks or fewer cars. Girls of this age hope for increased leisure facilities and better shops. They are concerned about personal violence, whereas boys of 14 appear to be no longer concerned about it. The pattern is similar for the global community. Both boys and girls hope for a world without war, although at primary school age both war and disasters are more of a concern to boys. All hope for an end to poverty and global pollution.

Their concerns for the local and global communities may be similar but boys and girls choose very different scenarios for their preferred futures. Nearly three-quarters of girls overall choose a future based on environmental concern, compared with half the boys. Boys are very attracted to a future dominated by new technology and 40% opt for this, as opposed to 19% of girls. This is endorsed by the writing and drawing of the pupils, in which many boys envisage a socially just but high tech future while girls want a world characterised by social justice, peacefulness, a clean environment and a protected countryside. The exception to this is the youngest children. 7 year old boys appear less attracted to new technology than older boys; indeed 7 year old girls choose this scenario twice as often as boys do. By 11, it appears that gender socialisation and the media have helped to give boys a one-dimensional technological view of the future.

With regard to gender, half of all the pupils feel that there will be greater equality for women in the future, and 40% think it will be the same as today. Slightly more girls than boys are positive about the possibility of increased gender equality, with secondary school pupils being the most optimistic. Given that pupils are not generally optimistic about conditions improving in the future for anyone other than themselves, this is significant as the one area where pupils feel progress is being made. It mirrors the feeling among many pupils that racial prejudice will also decrease as people's attitudes change.

What implications might be drawn from these findings for the curriculum? Certainly it is worrying that so few 18 year old boys feel they can do anything to help create a better future, and that boys have less interest in the future than girls. There is also a dichotomy in their preferred futures: many boys are attracted by new technology and yet in discussion show that they are aware of its negative effects — many lay the blame for unemployment on new technology. Boys *do* want a more just and equitable society and many hope for greater environmental awareness, but they accept a high tech future as inevitable and see it as an answer to all human problems. Girls, however, are more sceptical of the value of such a future, putting greater emphasis on people and relationships and less on technology. This emphasis on good relationships seems healthy and has implications for the curriculum in terms of providing more time for discussion of personal issues and co-operative group work for both boys and girls. Clearly, however, girls do also need to be able to engage confidently with technology at all levels.

It is interesting that while feminist writers maintain that girls are still disadvantaged by the educational system (eg Arnot, 1993), it appears that it is boys who feel more disempowered as future citizens at the age of 18. This is not to deny the existence of inequality and the dominance of patriarchy within the educational system, but only to acknowledge that boys seem to be struggling more than girls to maintain a sense of purpose in the face of massive change. Mac an Ghaill (1994) argues that boys are under great pressure to conform to a range of 'macho' student masculinities and that little time is given in schools for boys to explore differing views of what it is to be male in today's society. It would seem that the boys' attitudes in our survey towards technology and adult roles are part of this learned male culture. This would endorse Mac an Ghaill's findings that there is an urgent need for both teachers and pupils to re-assess the male values embedded in the education system.

The main findings of this research, then, are that from a very early age there are clear gender differences in attitudes towards the future and that these continue throughout the years of schooling. Boys and girls have very different perspectives about the world they would like and the part they feel they can play. Both sexes need to be given the time and encouragement to explore differing views of the future, and their roles as active citizens within that future. They need to be helped to challenge their assumptions and to listen to each others' point of view.

Implications for schools

Whilst pupils' specific hopes and fears vary according to their age, what is consistent is their concern about the future and their wish to consider this more seriously at school. Their personal future, the future of the local area and global issues are all seen as important but none, they say, is given adequate space in the curriculum. The examples of individual schools taking an issue seriously, e.g. studying racial prejudice in Religious Education, suggest that teaching and discussion can influence the development of children's attitudes.

Primary schools

Teachers in primary schools need to address all three dimensions of this research if they are to help children articulate their hopes and fears. Firstly, they need to acknowledge children's personal hopes and fears, ensuring that there is space in the week (eg circle time) which allows for discussion about them. They also need to acknowledge the anxiety felt by many children who are unsure about the images projected in stories and the media. Being able to differentiate between reality and fantasy is part of growing up. From time to time, stories read in the primary school need to model possible futures and enable children to explore their own ideas. The evidence of early gender stereotyping suggests the need to present alternative careers for both men and women and alternative versions of family life. Topics on 'jobs', 'people who help us' and 'families' can depict men and women in non-stereotyped roles.

Secondly, teachers need to be aware of the interest of primary age pupils in their local community and related social issues. The local area is studied as part of geography or history. Primary school children are very concerned about the future well-being of their local area, and local studies could be brought alive by building on this interest. Pupils are particularly concerned about environmental issues and these fit well into local studies. If the study can involve children in active work to improve the local area, this has the added advantage of building on children's enthusiasm and helping them realise that they themselves have a part to play as citizens of their community. In turn this will help them to feel able to take a role in shaping the future as young adults. So it is important that the curriculum emphasis in the National Curriculum on distant places does not marginalise study of the local area.

The concern of 11 year olds about social issues in the community extends to a fear of rising violence and crime, and drug and cigarette addiction. Time needs to be given to tackling these issues at the time that children feel positive about rejecting them, not leaving it until secondary school. Previously held assumptions that children of 11 were too young to be aware of sexual violence or drug addiction and that consequently it was an area which did not concern them clearly do not hold. Children are worried about these issues and would welcome more discussion about them.

Finally, primary school children's interest in the world around them, both immediate and other places, endorses Weigand's argument (1995) that geography should include the study of distant places and the local environment from an early age. The emphasis in the National Curriculum on distant places is therefore welcomed, although few of the 7 year olds in this survey indicate that they have had much geography teaching relating to distant places. Knowledge of other countries appears patchy and confused, but the interest is there. Even the 11 year olds appear to have learnt more about the history of countries than the geography. This may reflect the nature of the geography National Curriculum documents and the greater emphasis on history currently found in primary schools.

History inevitably has more to say about the past than the future but our research does have implications for this subject area. Between the ages of 7 and 11, children acquire a fear of war and an expectation that it may happen in the future. This may be partly as a result of history topics which depict war as a fact of life (Hutchinson, 1994). If conflict and war in the past are studied then equal time needs to be given to examples of peace-keeping and peace-building. It is also important to encourage children to envisage their own future so that they can maintain and build on their positive approach to life — through creative writing for example. The real missing link, however, is that children are not helped to see how environmental and socio-economic conditions can be changed. Many schools have charity days, but this approach can be superficial and lead to an assumption that giving money to the poor is the way to solve issues of poverty and hunger. Children also need to look at the underlying causes of such conditions and read some of the many materials exploring the issues (eg Oxfam and DEA educational resources). The cross-curricular theme, Education for Citizenship, acknowledges that children must be taught how to be active citizens, aware of how society changes and the part they can play. A study of organisations and people active in working for a better future should be central to such learning.

The stance taken by teachers is crucial. Both Education for Citizenship and Education for Industrial Understanding have been criticised for being too conservative, too concerned to maintain the status quo and the values of a capitalist economy (Hyland, 1991; Holden and Smith, 1993). A teacher may incorporate these themes in her teaching and never touch on issues relating to the creation of a more just society. On the other hand, the documents provide a framework for teachers prepared to take a socially critical approach to learning, to challenge current values and examine possible future alternatives.

Secondary schools

Secondary teachers have in their schools young people who are very concerned about their personal future but increasingly doubtful about whether they can really play a part in improving society in any way. They show an interest in their local community but say issues related to it have rarely been discussed in school. They do not appear to have been given the opportunity to discuss concerns such as unemployment or immigration, or at least not in a way that has helped them to move beyond simplistic explanations and stereotypical responses.

Pupils' perceptions of the curriculum are that they have been given only a superficial introduction to global issues. They feel they have received little or no citizenship education and have had few chances to discuss wider ethical issues. If these young people are not to become disillusioned, more time needs to be given in the secondary curriculum to such issues, particularly in personal and moral education. Most subject areas can contribute. History could include discussion of the possibilities of war and peace in the future. Geography can look in more depth at probable and preferable futures, whether for different places or over environmental issues. Science and technology have a particular responsibility for exploring the social and ethical dilemmas raised by an uncritical promotion of high-tech solutions to current global problems. Technology needs to include discussion of both the advantages and disadvantages of current and future developments.

What images of the future are presented by young people's fiction today and how might English teachers help pupils think creatively and critically about the future? Increasing students' knowledge of such issues will make them better informed adults, able to contribute to debates about environment and development. Charity events bring particular issues to pupils' attention but it needs to be stressed that charity is at best a palliative and that the underlying causes of injustice and inequality require political and economic change. Contributing to charity can create a sense of having done something but, as pupils get older, schools need to look at ways of encouraging involvement in local planning, in environmental schemes, and in giving students responsibility for organising their own events to effect change. Citizenship and political education, gender roles and dis-cussion of prejudice and stereotyping need to be at the forefront of good personal and moral education. If this does not occur, the ill-informed pupils of today may become the misinformed voters of tomorrow.

Conclusions

What is the overall contribution of this research to our knowledge of children's views of the future? Are the children in this particular survey saying anything different from previous generations? In relation to gen-der, our research endorses Brown's findings (1984) that girls are more likely than boys to reject a technological future and that materialist values are 'endorsed by and large by males'. Brown worked only with secondary pupils but our research indicates that these differences are already estab-lished in primary school. As 7 year olds have been in school for less than two years, it is likely that such differences are the result of socialisation at home and via the media, rather than the result of schooling, but they may be reinforced in the classroom. As noted in chapter one, boys' and girls' toys, comics and television programmes carry different messages and teach different skills. That these influences affect young children's views of the future should not be surprising, but it does raise questions about the role of school in challenging such assumptions and beliefs.

The literature on feminist futures discussed in chapter two suggests that women's visions of the future are more likely to highlight environmental concern and the importance of working together to create a more just society. Certainly the findings from this research would support greater emphasis on the importance of relationships and relating, on action for the future, and greater concern for the environment. It appears that secondary school reinforces the gender divide and that by the time they leave school, boys and girls have differing expectations about the future and different skills for coping with it. Schools need to look at ways of lessening this gap.

The research reviewed in chapter 3 shows that from the 1950s onwards several common themes have emerged in relation to children's views of the future. Our research endorses the findings of Gillespie and Allport (1955) and the later work of Johnson (1987). Like the US students in Johnson's work, British children in the 1990s envisage a fairly traditional lifestyle (house, car, partner) and think the future will be better than their lives are now. Also in keeping with US students, they are pessimistic about conditions improving for the majority of people in their local community and even more pessimistic about life improving for people in the rest of the world. They are more optimistic, however, than the Australian teenagers studied by Hutchinson (1993), who felt negative and helpless about both local and global issues. This may be a reflection of the wider age span of our research group — the optimism of the younger pupils inevitably influenced the overall findings — but even so our teenagers do not appear quite so pessimistic.

To conclude, British young people in the 1990s appear optimistic about their own future. They are committed to the responsibilities of adult life and wish for a good job, a good education and secure relationships with partners and children. They are less optimistic about the future for other people, both in their local community and globally. They are concerned about environmental destruction, growing crime and violence and social inequality and they fear that all will worsen. It is only in relation to attitudes over race and gender equity that they expect improvement.

Whatever future pupils hope for, be it characterised by environmental concern or high technology, they do not generally expect it to come about. They fear that the world will be essentially the same or worse than today. Whilst some pupils feel they can act on a personal level to help create a better future, many do not. They feel that school has given them an inadequate education in this area and that they would like more information, discussion and advice. They feel responsible as citizens of the future for what may happen, but lack a clear vision of what their own part in this might be and the knowledge of groups and organisations working for change. Pupils appear to have been given few strategies for coping with the widespread change in their lives and in society. While they often hope for a more just and sustainable future, school provides little opportunity for discussion on such issues. Their visions thus remain fragmented, and essentially conservative in a time of radical change.

PART THREE — TEACHING FOR TOMORROW

Chapter 7

A Futures Perspective

Educational institutions are already involved in preparing youth for their future, which will be very different from that experienced by previous generations. However, the missing element in this process is the inclusion of a definite futures perspective in the curriculum... A futures perspective is recommended in all disciplines, not as a 'bolt-on' but as a way of thinking. — The Wiltshire Report

With the curriculum in many industrialised countries being fore-closed in the interests of standardisation there is a very real danger that a futures perspective will remain forever a marginal educational concern. However the most innovative curriculum developments often come from the margins of the system where creativity and critical thinking are less restricted. This chapter describes initiatives in Britain and Australia which focus directly on the need to develop future-orientated skills in schools. Both initiatives are on-going and what is described here is a snapshot of 'work in progress.' The chapter also begins to answer the question 'What does a futures perspective in the curriculum actually look like?'

CHOICES FOR BRITAIN

In July 1994 *The Independent,* a UK daily newspaper, carried a headline which read 'Britain's future should be seen and heard'. The Editorial comment and a lengthy page two article both described the outcomes of an innovative curriculum project.

British schoolchildren want the country to take a more active role in Europe even at the expense of national independence, according to an experimental in-depth opinion survey. Many also felt Britain should cut back on international involvements and concentrate more on problems at home.

Choices for Britain was the first poll of its kind in the United Kingdom. More than 2000 pupils between 14 and 19 at schools in Avon took part in the pilot project. They were asked what they wanted Britain to be like in a decade. The aim was to give students an opportunity to discuss and learn about policy issues, before sampling opinion (*Independent,* 1994).

Background

The project had its origins in the work of an international, non-partisan, research and public education organisation concerned with foreign policy issues, called Saferworld. Part of Saferworld's brief was to promote informed and balanced discussion among young people on key questions relating to the security debate. They decided to work with students of 14 to 18 in the Bristol area.

What the project aimed to do through its methodology was to promote a range of life-skills related to communication, decision-making, and working with others. It also analysed students' opinions about possible futures for Britain, both those offered by the project and those identified by the students themselves. Some thirty schools and colleges took part in the pilot project which lasted from 1991-94. Nearly 3000 young people used the project's materials, roughly one in 20 of the 14-18 year olds in full-time state education in Avon (*Public Voice International,* 1994).

Generally the materials were used in personal and social education classes, General Studies and tutorials, as well as a range of subject areas. Teachers generally spent about four hours using the materials, following the suggestions laid out in the accompanying Teacher's Guide (Saferworld, 1993a). A large number of the participating teachers felt that Choices for Britain could be used as a basis for assessment in English, History and Geography.

Use in schools

The materials

The materials for students took an attractive tabloid A3 format with eight pages of text, maps, figures, cartoons and diagrams (Saferworld, 1993b). The text of the front page is shown in Table 7.1.

The pack gives outline information on Britain's past and present and identifies five threats to Britain's future. These are: problems at home, environmental problems, Britain's declining power, poverty in the world, conflicts and wars. Four scenarios follow for the year 2003, entitled: Great Britain, Euro-Britain, Global Britain and Island Britain. For each there is a brief description of what critics and supporters say, whether the scenario is realistic and how much it would cost. Examples of two of the scenarios are given below.

A range of activities follow, designed to encourage students to consider the different steps that would be required to reach each of the four futures. Finally, they are invited to complete a short questionnaire on how they feel about these futures. They are asked about whether they think the future will be better or worse, what they feel are the most serious threats to Britain and what Britain should do. They rank the four futures in order of preference and lastly, indicate what a fifth future, *their* future for Britain, would look like. Some of the questions for them to consider are:

— What do you believe are the most important problems facing Britain and the world?

— What kind of a country would you like Britain to be in ten years' time?

— Why would some people not like your future, and how would you respond to them? What are some good points about your future?

Table 7.1 — Choices for Britain

Choices for Britain

It's Your Future

What kind of future do you want to live in? What kind of country would you like Britain to be ten years from now?

Thinking seriously about Britain's future means deciding what we really value and why. It involves asking some tough questions.

- What are the problems facing Britain today?

- What should we do about them?

- What should we do about problems in other parts of the world?

- How should we be involved with the rest of Europe?

There are no simple answers, and it may not be easy to reach agreement. Some very difficult choices have to be made. At Saferworld, we think its time young people had a greater say about what kind of future they would like to see for Britain. To help you think through these important issues, we have prepared Choices for Britain.

First we invite you to think about how Britain has changed over the years and to examine what state our country is in today. Then you will see four different visions of Britain in ten years' time — the year 2003. When you've considered and discussed these four Futures, we ask you to let us know your opinions by completing a questionnaire.

Finally, you're invited to suggest a Future of your own — your vision of where you think Britain should be heading and how we might get there. Early next year, after young people throughout Avon and beyond have given their opinions, the results will be presented to politicians and the media. By thinking through what kind of future you want to see for Britain, you will be doing your part to help our country decide how to face the challenges of the 21st century.

Table 7.2 — Two scenarios

Great Britain

It is 2003. Over the past ten years, we have come to understand that the UK still has a special role to play in the world as an active and independent country. We are taking an active role in promoting freedom, democracy and fair play in other countries, for we know that Britain has a special responsibility to make the world a better place. We have kept our armed forces the same size and we send them to other countries when we feel we must, to help keep the peace. At home, we have worked hard to make our country's economy stronger. The rest of Europe may be working towards having common armed forces, a common foreign policy and a common currency, but we know that there would be more to lose than to gain by joining a United Europe. It would get us too involved in their own problems and prevent us from doing whatever we wanted around the world. So we have kept our freedom of action, though we continue to co-operate and do business with the rest of Europe. In 2003, we are a proud and powerful country, respected by our neighbours. We have made Britain great again.

Global Britain

It is 2003. Over the past ten years, we have come to understand that the world's problems are our problems. We knew that if the UK didn't do more about the growing poverty, pollution and conflicts in other parts of the world, and encourage other countries to do more too, these problems would seriously threaten us. To help narrow the gap between rich and poor countries, Britain now spends a great deal more each year on development assistance. We have also decided to forget about the money that many developing countries owe us. For a fairer world, we encourage the United States, Japan and other developed countries to allow developing countries more of a say in how the world is run. We work closely with the UN on global problems, and often provide our troops to help the UN keep the peace where there are conflicts. And we never use our own troops unless the UN approves. At home, we use our cars less and pay heavy taxes on products that cause pollution. Bananas and other foods from developing countries cost more, now that we are paying their farmers a fairer price. In 2003, Britain is working towards a bright new future for the world.

The Choices approach

The methodology used by the project was developed during the 1980s in the US and involves students in a five-step process described as follows (*Public Voice International*, 1994).

1. Introduction to the topic at hand.

2. Discussion and debate of a balanced set of values-oriented alternatives for action, framed as four future scenarios.

3. Completion of a special questionnaire/ballot ranking the alternatives.

4. Design of an alternative 'Future 5' reflecting personal values.

5. Production of a personal or group action plan.

These steps, it is suggested, enable students to develop valuable skills for life and the workplace, to challenge and clarify their own values, to engage in practical decision-making, to look at the 'big picture,' and the process empowers them to take positive action.

Throughout each step the primary role of the teacher is to act as an impartial chairperson, although no instructions are given for how this might best be done. The choice of four futures that students are given to work with are described as follows (Saferworld, 1993a):

> This balanced set of four alternative scenarios for the UK in 2003 has been carefully designed to reflect the variety of opinion around fundamental issues facing Britain's future: its relationship with the other countries of Europe and the world; its freedom of action; the relative importance of various national and international problems and how to solve them; and the degree and way in which it aims to exercise a significant role in world affairs. Each Future bears particular advantages, disadvantages, risks, trade-offs, costs and near-term implications for action. In each of the scenarios, there has been a strong national consensus towards following a particular course of action embodying a particular set of values. Collectively, the four Futures represent a broad range of current public opinion.

Although classroom debate on the advantages and disadvantages of each scenario is essential, it does not necessarily follow — as the materials seem to imply — that a process of values clarification will also occur.

Knowing the pros and cons is only one step towards analysing the underlying values debates. The materials do not say, however, what these value differences actually are or how they might be more explicitly explored.

Pilot evaluation

Teachers' responses

All the respondents said that they had enjoyed using the materials, that they found them helpful, and not an extra burden on their workload. Most, but not all, felt that the materials tied in well with existing classroom activities. Teachers noted a high level of student enjoyment and engagement in the futures debate. They commented that working with the materials raised students' awareness of world issues and other people's attitudes, as well as improving their ability to debate and relate to each other. Many observed that the most powerful motivator was asking pupils for *their* opinions on issues (*Public Voice International*, 1994). One teacher commented:

> I like the way it doesn't patronise them and it's very informative; we've had a lot of thoughtful responses. Last week, we had teachers of other subjects coming up and saying that students had been to them and told them what they had been doing in their Choices lessons, which I find quite extraordinary; I've never known that before! I think they like being asked for their opinions, and we've been stressing that their opinions are valued, and that they are the citizens of the future, and they've really taken to this.

Among the suggestions for improvement made by teachers were more imaginative ideas for using the materials, the inclusion of more contentious issues such as racism and poverty, and a set of more subject-specific back-up materials. Overall, teachers obviously valued and enjoyed the opportunity to try out these materials in their classrooms.

Students' responses

Students from six of the participating schools completed a questionnaire about their response to the materials. Half said that they enjoyed using them, a quarter said that they were OK, and another quarter didn't enjoy using them. Those who enjoyed using them did so because they valued the opportunity to express their opinions, they appreciated doing something different, and they learnt about new concerns. For example:

I liked Choices for Britain because it was a chance for us (the future generation) to put forward our views of the country.

I liked Choices because I think we have a right to say how we want the world to be.

I think it made pupils think more about the future. It also helped us to learn about Europe.

Those who didn't enjoy using the materials spoke of too many questions and too many lessons spent on the project. Some said that it wouldn't actually lead to any real change in the world.

One of the questions asked whether students felt differently about themselves, the class or their role as citizens, as a result of engaging in these debates. A number of students wrote about their increased involvement in class and a greater awareness of the issues.

I feel differently about myself now, because I think I took an active part in the discussion, and spoke in front of the whole class.

It made me realise how definite and how confused my political views are.

It made me decide what I want the world to be like and what sort of world I want to bring my children up into.

Choice of Futures

Over 2000 students completed the ballot sheets asking about their preferred Future scenario. The evaluation report (*Public Voice International,* 1994) comments:

Young people in Avon are extremely concerned about the state of their country, and believe that addressing national problems such as crime, homelessness and the economy should be a top priority. Yet they are also very concerned about environmental problems at home and abroad. They are pessimistic about the future of Britain and the world...

All four Futures for Britain attracted considerable support. The most popular future was Euro-Britain, followed by Island Britain, Global Britain, and Great Britain. 54% of students ranked Euro-Britain first or second in their ballots. But even Great Britain, in fourth place, was ranked first or second by almost 40% of students...

Slightly more than half of the respondents felt that Britain, and the world, will be a worse place in which to live in ten years time. Almost one third felt that the situation in both Britain and the world will remain the same, while less than one sixth felt it would improve.

The wider curriculum

There was a large measure of agreement among teachers about the value of Choices for skills development. In particular, they mentioned communication skills, decision-making skills, and the ability to work with others. There was unanimous agreement that Choices tied in with the needs of the National Curriculum, especially in English, History and Geography. One of the participating schools was using Choices during an official inspection which lead to considerable positive discussion with one inspector. Amongst the cross-curricular themes, Choices was considered particularly relevant to Education for Citizenship, Economic and Industrial Understanding and Environmental Education. Representatives from business and industry attended some sessions and were favourable impressed by what they saw and its relevance to the world of work.

Next steps

Partly due to the success of the Choices for Britain pilot project, a new educational organisation has been set up called Public Voice International. Its task is to produce formal and informal educational materials for young people and adults, focusing on a range of issues, such as the environment, crime, racism, AIDS, and the future of Europe. The purpose of these materials, as with Choices for Britain, will be to offer a range of viewpoints on such issues and to encourage wider debate about their resolution, leading to identification of new visions, solutions and appropriate practical goals.

Several new projects are already in their early stages. After the Avon pilot comes the national Choices for Britain project. This will include publication of student materials and a teachers' guide. A second project, which could be replicated elsewhere, is Choices for Bristol, which will focus on a set of alternative scenarios for the city in 2005. Its findings will result in a picture of how the people of Bristol would like their city to be in the twenty-first century. Thirdly, Choices for Sustainability will explore the question 'What would a sustainable society look like, and how do we get there?' The outcomes of this project will be used to support Local Agenda 21 programmes arising out of the 1992 Earth Summit. Fourthly, Racism: What Is It Good For?, will be run in collaboration with the Commission for Racial Equality. It will enable participants to share experiences, explore different viewpoints, and consider appropriate responses to racism. It will be promoted through community groups, trade unions, religious groups, youth clubs and other organisations.

Public Voice International thus marks a new initiative and development in public education. Its emphasis on community consultation, opinion analysis, civic empowerment and policy development, comes just at a time when, more than ever before, 'public imagination, commitment and energy (needs to) be tapped more effectively if we are to create a better future'. (Berger, 1994). Enthusiasm for such initiatives is clearly present in society, as the Avon project has shown. One wonders how it will fare with a wider student and adult audience.

One of the dissonant features of these programmes so far is that they emphasise the use of futures scenarios but neglect wider insights from futures education and futures studies. There is a wealth of international expertise which, if properly used, could conceptually enhance and ground this work. Such an infusion would both increase its effectiveness and sharpen its recommendations.

CHOICES FOR AUSTRALIA

Introduction

During the last ten years Australia has been the scene of many exciting curriculum innovations, especially in socially critical fields such as peace education, global education and education for sustainability. During the 1990s attention has turned to the need for a much clearer futures dimension in the school curriculum. In part this has been encouraged by the setting up of a Commission for the Future, which has worked to promote a wider debate about the future in Australia.

Education in Australia differs from Britain in that each state has control over its own education system. In Australia, moreover, denominational and private schools make up a much larger sector of the educational community and teachers' unions and subject organisations play a larger part in curriculum development. This gives greater scope for interesting curriculum initiatives but these may remain localised or confined to one state. The latter part of this chapter describes two current initiatives in the state of Queensland.

Shaping the Future

This is the title of an official Queensland government report on the secondary school curriculum (Wiltshire, 1994), which made specific reference to education for the future. The purpose of this report was to review the whole school curriculum and to make recommendations to the state government. These are currently under consideration and, of course, might not all be supported.

One chapter in the third volume of the report, 'Futures and the Curriculum' (O'Rourke, 1994) sets out to:

— examine the current literature in Futures Studies

— develop understanding about what is meant by Futures Studies

— develop understanding of strategies and tactics available for managing change through Futures Studies

— review the issue of Futures Studies in development of policy nationally and internationally

— review futures-based curricula in terms of possible subjects for/of the future and also futures-based subjects.

O' Rourke comments:

> It is argued that 'In Australia we can no longer count on being the 'lucky country' or merely aspire to being the 'clever country'. Creative generation of alternative futures can assist decision makers by increasing awareness and contributing at least partially to understanding complex situations, and can assist in bringing about change from the present Australian context to a preferred future context.

The main elements of this chapter (O'Rourke, 1994) are described below.

Key concepts

It is suggested that understanding the future is enhanced by learning to conceptualise it in different ways. Five examples of 'concepts from the literature' are given.

Vision — the importance of creating and enhancing vision as a means for setting goals for the future, whether in one's personal life, at work, in education or nationally.

Changing society — changes in society today are creating turbulence in the present and make consideration of a range of alternative possible futures even more important.

Alternative futures — being clearer about possible future alternatives, both probable and preferable, enhances decision-making in the present and helps people to deal with change more effectively.

Sustainability — importance is increasingly being given to the need to create a more sustainable future society and exploration of sustainability is now a vital part of many environmental and economic debates.

Methodologies — a variety of strategies are available to generate insights into the future, ranging from brainstorming, futures wheels, cross-impact matrices and scenarios, to trend analysis and extrapolation, Delphi studies and scanning.

The development of policy

When rapid change becomes the norm, the quality of decision makers' choices becomes even more important than before. Examples are given of this at international, national and state scales. The achievement of satisfactory futures requires major improvements in policy-making, governance and public administration.

Realisation of the extent of change and the need for forward planning has led to investigation of future scenarios for Australia in the twenty-first century. Four major scenarios proposed by the Commission for the Future (1989) are: i) More growth, but modestly; ii) Shift to the Right — Australian Thatcherism; iii) Left is still best — planned economy; and iv) Smaller and sustained futures — new paradigm.

Bernadette O'Rourke goes on to say that 'An examination of Queensland Department of Education documents (also) shows an increasing realisation of the need for vision in education as an overarching philosophy'. She cites various studies which stress the need for vision but notes that they generally fail to articulate what that vision might be. Again the use of alternative future scenarios, this time in relation to educational policy, would be one way of sharpening discussion and debate about appropriate priorities.

Futures in the curriculum

This section of the report examines the curriculum possibilities for more specific exploration of the future and gives case studies of good practice. It is suggested that a 'free-standing futures subject' needs to be developed as a priority to aid integration of futures perspectives into other disciplines. An example of such a syllabus, it is noted, is being considered by the Board of Senior Secondary School Studies (see below).

Next, examples are given of the integration of futures into school curricula. Some of the students doing geography at Corinda State High School were sceptical at first but one commented later:

> Well, I think that, you know, before I did the course on the future, you don't give much thought to it, but it's made me aware of possible outcomes that might happen in twenty-five years. I haven't given it much thought, whether it's going to affect me or not... It's just made me aware... the future's coming, we have to look ahead now, to predict, to plan, to make sure we get something... (O'Rourke, 1994).

The report concludes with comments on pedagogy and school organisation and the appendices include an outline model futures curriculum. The recommendations relating to a futures concern in the curriculum are found in volume one of the report (Wiltshire, 1994).

Recommendations

These are the recommendations to the Queensland government relating to a futures dimension in the curriculum.

1. Every syllabus to have a futures perspective so as to provide a dynamic, proactive and responsive curriculum that will prepare our youth for the 21st century.

2. Every syllabus to have critical-thinking skills included so as to provide a sound basis for the problem-solving and decision-making that is essential in futures study. Relevant elements of each syllabus should seek to develop higher order thinking, creative solutions and problem solving.

3. Educational organisations, whether they be at state, regional or school level, to work to a clearly stated vision that is shared by all stakeholders, with possible, preferable and probable alternative futures considered.

4. A futures perspective to be included in pre-service teacher education courses as well as being embedded in the in-service programs for the new syllabus.

5. Queensland's new curriculum structures to have a strong research base, with good international and Australia-wide links, along with periodic reviews of curriculum content and process to keep abreast of change.

A Futures Curriculum

The review of the Queensland school curriculum was carried out in order to make recommendations to the government. The second initiative to be described here specifically sets out to create curriculum change. If successful it could play an important part in implementing the above recommendations regarding futures in the curriculum.

The Queensland Catholic Education Commission has an interest in global and futures education and drafted a syllabus for upper secondary pupils called Futures: Personal, Social and Global. This was submitted to the Queensland Board of Senior Secondary School Studies for wider accreditation. At first the Board nearly turned down the syllabus but its originators argued that the committees lacked expertise in the futures field. To their credit, the Board set up an ad hoc advisory committee with relevant expertise in early 1994.

Recommendations

This Futures Committee was charged with setting parameters for the development of a draft syllabus in Futures, listing the criteria by which such a syllabus could be evaluated, and reviewing the syllabus submitted to the Board. It recommended that:

1. That a Senior syllabus in Futures be developed by the Board of Senior Secondary School Studies in accordance with the advice provided through review of the (submitted) syllabus.

2. That the Futures subcommittee be reconstituted to ensure a percentage of members has expertise in Futures.

3. That the further development of the syllabus be determined through observance and use of (agreed) parameters and criteria.

The original syllabus submitted by the Queensland Catholic Education Commission thus played a crucial role in setting this process in motion. Its author (Rundall, 1994) noted that 'whereas the new Board course will be a course with integrity and worth, it will be more conservative, more prescribed and more content based.' However, submitting the original syllabus to review and critique by experts in the futures field, made it into a more rigorous document. The committee formed to write the new syllabus completed their task early in 1995. An indication of the final curriculum content is given by Slaughter's (1994) draft outline, included in the Appendix to the Futures Committee Report (Galbraith, 1994). Its main elements are described in shortened form in Table 7.3.

How different the final syllabus to be written by the Futures Committee will be, remains to be seen. What is offered here is a glimpse of the *sort* of objectives and learning experiences that it may well offer. Certainly it is clear that a specific Futures curriculum is needed if these issues are to be adequately dealt with in the upper secondary school. While each subject area has a specific contribution to make to the overall future dimension in the curriculum, *this* provides the core experience. A new century is a good time to reflect on the need for new subjects to meet the needs of changing times.

The initiatives described in this chapter highlight the concerns of futures educators and also the different ways in which innovations may arise. It is interesting that both Choices for Britain and the original syllabus submission to the Queensland Catholic Education Commission came out of a deep interest in the future, but not expertise in or knowledge of futures studies. The Australian initiative takes a significant step forward in being grounded in this expertise. Will Public Voice International similarly choose to build on this experience?

Table 7.3 — A futures curriculum

Futures: Personal, Social and Global

Semester 1: Introduction to the Futures Field

Objectives

To introduce students to the knowledge-base of futures studies and some key applications of futures work.

To familiarise students with futures concepts, tools, imaging processes, organisations and the work of representative individuals.

To develop a foundation for the value skills, attitudes and competencies that are needed to explore and understand personal, social and global futures.

Learning experiences

Values clarification exercises.

Use of maps of the field to explore typical activities.

Overview of futures concepts and in-depth exploration of a selection of them.

Introduction to, and use of, simple methods and tools.

Investigation into the range, distribution and work of futures organisations (such as the World Future Society, the World Futures Studies Federation, the Club of Rome, the Australian Commission for the Future and other Institutes of Foresight).

Review the lives and work of exemplary futurists (eg. Robert Jungk, Hazel Hendeson, Elise Boulding, Jim Dator).

The role of short and long-term thinking in Australian society and culture (eg. politics, business, education).

How future discounting works.

The foresight principle: what it is and how it works.

Table 7.3 — A futures curriculum (continued)

Semester 2: Social Innovation and Personal Empowerment

Objectives

To explore the significance of social innovations in a range of contexts.

To develop personal empowerment and the skills to act as an agent of change.

To understand the links between personal empowerment and social innovation, and also the responsibilities involved.

To practice the skills appropriate to the design, planning, implementation and evaluation of a change project.

Learning experiences

Survey of past social innovations in two different cultures.

Case study of recently successful social innovations (eg. the emancipation of women, environmental protection, the peace movement).

Study of unsuccessful innovations. Investigation of why they failed.

Plan of future innovation using the Change Cycle.

Personal/group empowerment work.

Table 7.3 — A futures curriculum (continued)

Semester 3: State of the Planet

Objectives

To develop a global overview of the state of the planet.

To understand the implications of major trends, issues, problems and alternatives.

To develop a clear view of possible solutions and the role of individuals, organisations and governments in implementing them.

Learning experiences

Practical work on exponential growth using micro-organisms, simulations, historical examples.

Case studies of growth in finite systems. Case studies of islands (eg. Bermuda, Madagascar, Tasmania).

Modelling the dynamics of growth (using World3 — Meadows).

Comparing/contrasting different conceptions of growth (eg. quantitative and qualitative, material and non-material).

Personal health criteria (as starting point) and the relevance of health in the context of the global system.

What might sustainability mean?

What might a sustainable society look like?

Focus on specific problems and issues (eg. global warming, tropical forests, economic and trade imbalances, population growth etc).

Table 7.3 — A futures curriculum (continued)

Semester 4: Paths to Sustainability

Objectives

To explore the meaning of sustainability in relation to human culture and its global environment.

To understand the main impediments to achieving sustainability.

To appreciate and develop competence in the range of personal and social processes contributing to the above.

To explore means of moving towards sustainability in specific areas.

Learning experiences

The 'megatrends' approach and why it failed.

Critiques of standard economic assumptions.

Aspects of 'the new economics.'

Redefining growth.

How human and technical impacts may be reduced.

Planning for sustainability — Australian and overseas examples.

Re-evaluating industrial-era beliefs, practices and ethics.

The ethical foundations of stewardship and intrinsic value.

Barriers and impediments to sustainability.

Social innovations and sustainability: what individuals, groups and governments can do.

Assembling an outline 'map' of the early 21st century.

Developing an agenda for the 21st century.

Chapter 8

Looking Forwards

Students in the next century will need to know how to create a civilisation that runs on sunlight, conserves energy, preserves biodiversity, protects soils and forests, develops sustainable local economies and restores the damage inflicted on the Earth. In order to achieve such ecological education we need to transform our schools and universities. — David Orr

This final chapter returns to the importance of positive visions of the future in times of rapid socio-cultural change. It begins by recalling the significance of images of the future, as set out in Part One of this book, and goes on to identify possible sources of inspiration and hope to support new visions. It concludes by highlighting the implications for education and, in particular, the importance of educating for a more sustainable future.

Visions for the future

In summary

This book has broken new ground in bringing together several hitherto disparate concerns which highlight new educational needs for the twenty-first century. It draws attention to the dilemmas of living in a period of rapid global change and stresses the critical role of education in such times. It has argued that education needs to have a much clearer focus on the future.

As the millennium approaches, interest in the future grows but most commentators fail to draw on the specific expertise of futurists and those working in the futures field. Futures research, futures studies and future-orientated social movements all offer powerful insights for educators. At the same time all views of the future are influenced by ideological assumptions which often need clearer acknowledgement. In particular, images of the future can play a crucial role in societal and cultural change.

Research on people's views of the future has been patchy and of variable quality. The main studies suggest that adults' images of the future are not well developed and are more likely to be pessimistic than optimistic. People generally feel they have little control over the future, a future more often than not seen solely in terms of developments in science and technology. Young people show high levels of concern about the future and are often fearful of what it will bring.

The UK study described in Part Two confirms many of these findings and adds significantly to our understanding of these issues. Young people's current hopes and fears for the future — personal, local and global — have been established, and account taken of variations based on age and gender. There seems less dissonance between personal and global expectations than some previous studies reported, possibly because life has become increasingly problematic at all levels of society in the late twentieth century.

We noted and explored examples of emerging good practice: Firstly, Choices for Britain, a project based in Bristol which works with older pupils using different scenarios for the future of Britain. Secondly, the Queensland review of the secondary curriculum, with its emphasis on the need for a clear futures dimension in schools. As a result of this a Futures syllabus has been prepared for use with senior pupils.

These developments show a growing convergence of interest between futurists and educators. Each has much to learn from the other. Futurists interested in education need to understand the daily reality of classroom life, the problems of curriculum development and current debates in education. Educators interested in making their teaching more future-orientated need not need 'reinvent the future' — futurists have already developed many practical ideas and activities that they can use. Some of the best work comes from those who see themselves as both futurists and educators.

Managing the millennium

Reference was made in chapter 1 to the approaching millennium and the way in which the change from one century to another activates an interest in the future. The end of a century frequently appears as a time of crisis, a socio-cultural rite of passage as it were, which stirs up deep longings and deep fears about the human condition. This should not be surprising since such times lend themselves to contemplation of 'ends' and 'beginnings.' Krishnan Kumar (1993) writes:

> 'Endism' is rampant, and likely to become even more so as we get closer to the end of the second millennium. Millennial endings, even more than centurial ones, give rise to millennial imaginings. But there is a profound difference between the millennial thoughts of our time and those of earlier ages.

Vita Fortunati, (1993) cites the current range of global dilemmas as presaging millennial changes which 'construct an exceptional sort of bridge with the future'. She draws particular attention to the myth of the Apocalypse as 'a brilliant metaphor for the human condition'. This long-held myth of the world's ending, she argues, depends on the juxtaposition of positive and negative elements: light versus dark, death versus rebirth, decadence versus regeneration. The myth of the Apocalypse taps into deep-seated human fears of separation, loneliness and death.

These are all themes which the current social and global crises help to highlight. They also help to underpin the psychology of despair described in the first chapter of this book. The times that we live in evoke hopelessness about the human condition and also hope for the possibility of new beginnings. We struggle with both, in different forms, in daily life, in society and on a global scale. Rather than succumbing to denial or despair we need to reconsider the crucial role of vision in such times.

The importance of vision

The title of this book stresses visions *of* the future, for that has been its main focus. It attempts to answer the question 'How do people in the West view the future of society and the planet?' In so doing the crucial importance of visions *for* the future also emerges. The images, views, visions that we already have tend to be fragmentary, one-dimensional, pessimistic and sometimes fearful. The visions that we *need*, if Polak's thesis is correct, (see chapter 3) are quite the opposite.

Positive images of the future offer hope and direction to individuals, institutions and wider society. But positive images cannot emerge out of thin air; there needs to be some substance, some stuff out of which they can be woven. We need to look for nodes, powerful ideas, inspirational events, social currents, which will encourage the crystallisation of such images.

Donella Meadows (1993) writes:

Visioning means imagining, at first generally and then with increasing specificity, what you really want. That is, *what you really want*, not what someone has taught you to want, and not what you have learned to be willing to settle for. Visioning means taking off all the constraints of assumed 'feasibility', of disbelief and past disappointments, and letting your mind dwell upon its most noble, uplifting, treasured dreams.

But, as the quotation at the beginning of this chapter indicates, vision on its own achieves little. The important symbiotic relationship is that between vision and action. Vision offers direction and energy because it harnesses deep aspirations. Direction and energy lead to effective work and action, which may in turn lead to modification of the vision. It may broaden it, also strengthen it. The test of any vision is whether it speaks to people's hearts, to their sense of compassion and justice, for both people and planet.

Duane Elgin (1991) observes that:

We cannot build a future we cannot imagine. A first requirement, then, is to create for ourselves a realistic, compelling, and engaging vision of the future that can be simply told. If our collective visualisation of the future is weak and fragmented, then our capacity to create a future together will be commensurately diminished. Without a strong sense of the future and meaningful orientation for our lives, we can lose confidence in ourselves, our leaders, and our institutions.

Whilst the broad task may be simply stated it is also fraught with difficulty. Fears are often seen as realistic and visions as idealistic and many people feel they lack the power to create real change in society. Where might one look for inspiration on this journey of the imagination?

Envisioning the future

The utopian tradition

There is in Western society a long tradition of utopian thought and practice which concerns itself with the nature of the 'good life' and the 'good society'. Sir Thomas More coined the term in 1516 as the title of his novel describing an ideal society. It is based on a pun in Greek, meaning both the good place (eutopia) and nowhere (outopia). The utopian imagination has been expressed principally in two ways. There is a *literary* tradition of utopian writing, which continues to the present day, and there is also a *lived* tradition of utopia, where different groups have set up community initiatives in order to live out their social and political ideals in daily practice.

The value of utopias lies in the fact that they make a detailed socio-political critique of existing society and also offer a blueprint, an ideal vision, for the future. Utopias also enrich our understanding because they attempt to take a holistic view of society in all its aspects rather than focusing on any one part. Krishnan Kumar (1991) argues that:

> Utopia's value lies not in relation to present practice but in its relation to a possible future. Its 'practical' use is to overstep the immediate reality to depict a condition whose clear desirability draws us on, like a magnet. Here the very visionary and 'impractical' quality of utopia is its strength.

There is, some commentators argue, 'a fundamental utopian propensity in human beings' (Levitas, 1990), something Robert Browning understood when he wrote, 'Ah, but a man's reach should exceed his grasp, or what's a heaven for?' Novels such as William Morris's *News From Nowhere*, written in 1890, Marge Piercy's *Woman on the Edge of Time*, (1976) Ernest Callenbach's *Ecotopia Emerging*, (1981) and Starhawk's *The Fifth Sacred Thing*, (1994) all offer incisive critiques of their time and powerful visions of preferable futures.

There are many examples of religious and political groups putting their utopian ideals into practice. These range from Gerrard Winstanley and the Diggers in the 17th century, Robert Owen the industrialist and his settlement at New Lanark in the 19th century, to the hippie communes of the 1960s. Some such experiments have been short-lived, others much longer. In particular they have provided the opportunity for people to try and live out their utopian ideals in practice. McLaughlin and Davidson (1985) have described in some detail the important role of intentional communities in this tradition and the way in which a deep yearning for community is an abiding element of the human condition.

It was Marx who gave utopia its pejorative connotation, when he distinguished his own scientific socialism from that of the earlier utopian socialists. They, he argued, lacked clear political analysis so to be utopian meant to be unrealistic. In 1917 many saw the Russian Revolution as the world's greatest utopian experiment. As its dictatorial nature became clear, some argued that utopianism had failed, an argument heard again in 1989 when the Soviet empire crumbled.

However, the utopian tradition is much more than this. It provides a well-spring of creativity which regularly manifests in both literary and lived form. In particular it emerges in times of socio-cultural upheaval when new visions are needed for the next cycle of change (Goodwin and Taylor, 1982). That we may currently be in just such a period is increasingly being recognised. Attention is therefore turning again to the insights and experiences that can be gained from this rich tradition.

New social movements

A second source of inspiration comes from the new social movements which have arisen since the 1960s. These have focused variously on issues such as human rights, peace, women, race, nuclear weapons, ecology, land rights. Examples include the Civil Rights movement in the USA and the anti-Vietnam war movement in the 60s, the women's movement, the Greenham Peace Camp, the anti-racist movement, the peace movement,

CND, and the environmental movement. Such social movements are a form of collective action which involves a strong sense of solidarity, common purpose and periodic mobilisation for political action aimed at creating fundamental social change (Scott, 1992).

Anyone who has been involved in such movements will know that they are often chaotic, diffuse, factionalised and marginalised. This is because they generally work outside established institutional frameworks and use a loose and non-hierarchical structure. While such movements display continuity over a period of time their visibility varies. For much of the time a movement may be invisible because in a latent phase. This is broken by periods of mobilisation on the streets and high visibility in the media.

Over time such social movements can have a significant impact on society. They play an important historical role in shaping the intellectual climate, acting as generators of new cultural values and alternative lifestyles. They challenge and therefore help to change existing social and political institutions, as with the absorption of Green demands or the creation of Green political parties. Similarly, the struggle for women's rights over the last twenty five years has become partially internalised in mainstream society.

Such social movements act as invisible cultural laboratories, their networks submerged in everyday life. Adherents try to live out the changes they seek to achieve in their own lives, acting as if they were experiments from the future that they desire. Such movements are generally aware of both the local and global dimension to their struggle. They stimulate radical questions, warn of crucial problems that are being ignored, often acting as antennae for society. They provide glimpses of possible futures and guidelines towards their realisation.

Reactionary forces, of course, portray such movements as at best irrational, if not downright dangerous to the effective functioning of society. Both struggle to control the future, but each is inspired by quite different visions of the future. In the long term it is the new social movements which offer inspiration and hope — for a society which is more ecologically responsible, less violent, valuing of gender and racial equality, less technologically hazardous and open to the needs of future generations.

Futures workshops

A small but important group of futurists have worked to revive the skills of envisioning which often seem to be so lacking in contemporary society. Robert Jungk and Norbert Mullert (1987), for example, worked with a variety of groups all over Europe to help them come up with new and imaginative proposals for action for the future. Jungk cites working with groups to update a school system, cut down on bureaucracy, solve the energy crisis, and opening a new youth centre. In each case he notes the need to work through people's feelings of disempowerment to re-connect with their often buried dreams of a better future. By drawing in his workshops on the intuitive and emotional as well as the rational and analytic, groups are able to identify new alternative visions and responses to their problems.

Similar work is carried out by Robert Ziegler (1989) who has published a series of workbooks on envisioning the future. Over many years of working with community, business and activist groups on their chosen futures, Ziegler has evolved a five-stage process (1991). This begins by focusing on the particular concerns of the group, moving on to individual imaging of the desired future, and then the creation of a shared vision. This shared vision is repeatedly refined and made more concrete and then related to the present by identifying appropriate strategies for action.

Elise Boulding (1988) worked with Ziegler in the 1980s to design workshops for helping peace activists envision a future without nuclear weapons. In working with other diverse groups she notes the re-occurring features of people's preferred futures: no age, gender or racial segregation; a non-hierarchical world; low profile technology; and people operating out of a more peaceable sense of awareness. What such workshops clearly indicate is that people *can* envision their preferable societal futures, given appropriate processes and procedures. Educators now need to consider the part such a process should play in personal and social education, citizenship and environmental education.

Implications for education

Socially critical education

For education to play a role in helping manage socio-cultural change it has to help teachers and learners face uncertainty and breakdown of meaning, while at the same time identifying new modes of understanding

142

for the new century. This requires an approach to education which is socially critical, open to new and radical insights, prepared to leave outmoded practice behind and to pioneer new ways of being and learning. Such an approach has a long tradition in the UK and elsewhere. John Fien (1993a) writes:

> The socially critical orientation in education is founded upon a belief in the need for education to play a role, along with other social institutions and agencies, in creating just and democratic societies. This orientation values the personal development and achievement objectives of liberal/progressive education. However, it also believes that they are insufficient educational goals in a world that is structurally unequal in terms of class, gender and race relations. Recognising that education can never be ideologically neutral, the socially critical orientation is committed to active pedagogical initiatives aimed at promoting social justice, equality and democracy.

This is the orientation of the new movements in education — global education, development education, peace education, and other allied initiatives — as described in chapter 1 (Lister, 1987). Examples of this in classroom format can be found in resources such as *Making Global Connections* (Hicks and Steiner, 1989) and *Reconnecting* (Pike and Selby, 1995). It is also the orientation of radical educators working within subject disciplines, for example Fien and Gerber's *Teaching Geography for a Better World* (1988). It is also the perspective of the authors of the present book.

Holding to a socially critical stance can be a particularly demanding task. Robin Richardson's 'essays, stories and memoranda' (1990) provide a graphic and inspiring account of the struggle to do this within the system. First as Adviser for Multicultural Education in Berkshire and then as Chief Inspector of Education in Brent, he experienced at first hand the possibilities and pitfalls of trying to promote social justice within official educational structures. The socially critical perspective will always be wilfully misunderstood by those who resist change and those with vested interests in maintaining the status quo.

In the UK the introduction of the National Curriculum focused attention on subject knowledge to the detriment of broader cross-curricular approaches. The teacher networks built up by those working in global

143

education and multicultural education, for example, became marginalised. Now that the National Curriculum has been slimmed down, it is
time to re-visit the broader ethical issues raised by radical educators.
Under what flag might such concerns now rally? The two main conten-
ders, we would argue, are futures education and education for sustainability. As far as schools and classrooms are concerned the two can be
merged into the key concept of 'sustainable futures'.

Education for sustainability

The Earth Summit in Rio focused attention on the crucial role of education
in promoting a more sustainable form of global development in all
countries.

> Formal education should not only be provided more widely but
> changed in content. Children and adults should be schooled in the
> knowledge and values that will allow them to live sustainably. This
> requires environmental education, linked to social education. The
> former helps people to understand the natural world, and to live in
> harmony with it. The latter imparts an understanding of human
> behaviour and an appreciation of cultural diversity. To date, this blend
> of environmental and social education has not been widely applied.
> It needs to be — at all levels (IUCN/UNEP/WWF, 1991).

Education for sustainability is not the sole preserve of environmental
educators, geographers or scientists, although each has a major contribution to make. Neither is it solely the prerogative of teachers of English,
Religious Education or personal and social education. The skills and
expertise of each need to be brought together in a major refocusing of
education to meet future needs.

Is this a bigger task than educators can manage? If schools merely
reflect the inequalities and the mores of consumerist society, why should
change here be easier than in any other sector of society? There is no
reason why it *should* be easier, but educators, of all professionals, should
be aware of the potential education has for catalysing change. The picture
we give of the world, whatever subject is taught, whatever age group,
matters enormously. Do we tell the old stories or do we look for a new
paradigm that better explains these times and the directions we need to
go in (Milbrath, 1989)?

Several writers on education and the environment are now identifying education, as traditionally practised, as a major element in the current global crisis. David Orr (1992) sums up the dilemma succinctly:

> Education in the modern world was designed to further the conquest of nature and the industrialisation of the planet. It tended to produce unbalanced, underdimensioned people tailored to fit the modern economy. Postmodern education must have a different agenda, one designed to heal, connect, liberate, empower, create, and celebrate.

Gregory Smith (1992) observes that much of the current debate about education focuses narrowly on the link between education and economic productivity, on the need for industrialised countries to be more competitive in the global market. This, he argues, is extremely short-sighted for it totally ignores the ecological limits to growth which may soon necessitate a decline in material production in the rich world.

> An educational process capable of helping children learn attitudes and forms of behaviour more in keeping with significantly changed material conditions will have to be informed with a worldview whose fundamental assumptions lead, not to the detachment characteristic of our own era, but to forms of identification, participation, commitment, and accountability recognising interdependence and interconnection with others (Smith, 1992).

Materials which begin to challenge the old forms of knowledge and which look towards more integrated ways of knowing are beginning to emerge in the educational community. The Australian Association for Environmental Education helped to produce *Teaching for a Sustainable World* (Fien, 1993b), a comprehensive range of workshops on environmental and development issues designed for teacher educators. The World Wide Fund for Nature UK has an in-service programme entitled 'Reaching Out', which explores issues of environmental education and education for sustainability. In Australia, Deakin University and Griffith University have an MEd programme which focuses on education and sustainability (Fien, 1993a) and South Bank University in London has a distance-learning MSc in Environmental and Development Education.

Epilogue

The end of the century and the new millennium will encourage all sorts of speculation about beginnings and endings. We live in volatile times where the past offers little guidance to the needs of tomorrow. As Giddens (1994) points out:

> Where the past has lost its hold, or become one 'reason' among others for doing what one does, pre-existing habits are only a limited guide to action; while the future, open to numerous 'scenarios', becomes of compelling interest.

Giddens (1990), an astute commentator on the consequences of modernity, argues that we urgently need to create 'models of utopian realism', models of the good society. Such utopian realism, he suggests, encompasses four dimensions. One axis links 'politicisation of the local' and 'politicisation of the global'. The other axis links 'life politics' to 'emancipatory politics'. Life politics is about personal self-actualisation, whereas emancipatory politics is about the politics of inequality. Local and global, personal and political, neither is complete without the other.

Such concerns have long been part of global education and are constantly being re-interpreted and updated to meet current needs (Steiner, 1995). Few educators have as yet begun to look holistically at the educational needs of the early twenty-first century. In a keynote address to the Australian Association for Environmental Education, Hicks (1993) suggested five questions that teachers need to ask in order to 'reclaim the future'.

Such questions need to be asked of all subject areas in the curriculum and at all levels of education.

Such questions are also part of the longer term ideological struggle centering on the purposes of education itself. As Bowers (1993) comments:

> One part of the ecological crisis where we have particular responsibility has to do with an ideology that equates personal identity and success with consumerism, and with possessing the symbols of power and social status. This drive to consume...further strengthens the ecologically destructive practices within our form of economy where the demand for growth in profits leads to creating new markets for a

continual stream of technological innovations. The insanity of living in a state of ecological imbalance has been...correctly identified in some quarters for what it is: namely, a crisis in the direction our spiritual development has taken over the course of the last four to five hundred years.

Such profound issues require a constant re-creation of education at all levels, from university and initial teacher education to schools and class-rooms and professional development. As the dust settles from the impo-sition of a National Curriculum, educators need to re-enquire as to their deepest hopes and dreams for themselves and their pupils. If, as Whitaker suggests (1995), 'successful education is more about vision, ambition and hope than it is about requirement, accountability and retribution', then we have exciting and challenging times ahead.

Table 8.1 — Reclaiming the future

When and where in my teaching do I encourage students to:

1. Share their feelings about the future as the third millennium approaches?

2. Learn about the crucial environmental and development issues which were debated at the Earth Summit?

3. Discuss the possible future impact of current global trends on their lives in the twenty-first century?

4. Listen to a range of different voices on the future, utopian and feminist, indigenous and Third World?

5. Explore the need for, and nature of, sustainable development in both the local and global community?

References

Albinski, N. (1988) *Women's Utopias in British and American Fiction*, London, Routledge

Arnot, M. (1993) 'A crisis in patriarchy? British feminist educational politics and state regulation of gender', in: Arnot, M. and Weiler, K. *Feminism and Social Justice in Education*, London, Falmer

Beardslee, W. and Mack, J. (1982) The impact on children and adolescents of nuclear developments, *Psychosocial Aspects of Nuclear Development*, Task Force Report No. 20, American Psychiatric Association

Beare, H. and Slaughter, R. (1993) *Education for the Twenty-First Century*, London, Routledge

Bell, W. and Mau, J. (1971) *The Sociology of the Future*, New York, Russell Sage Foundation

Berger, K. (1994) Personal communication from project co-director

Boulding, E. (1978) The dynamics of imaging futures, *World Future Society Bulletin*, 12 (5), pp.1-8

Boulding, E. (1988) *Building a Global Civic Culture: Education for an Interdependent World*, London, Teachers College Press

Boulding, E. (1988) 'Image and action in peace building', chapter 5 in: Hicks, D. ed. (1994) *Preparing for the Future: Notes and Queries for Concerned Educators*, London, Adamantine Press

Bowers, C.A. (1993) *Education, Cultural Myths, and the Ecological Crisis*, Albany, State University of New York Press

Boyer, K. (1989) Teaching and Learning About Futures, MA in Educational Studies, University of York

Brown, L. (1993) 'A new era unfolds', chapter 1 in: *State of the World 1993*, Worldwatch Institute, London, Earthscan Publications

Brown, M. (1984) Young people and the future, *Educational Review*, 36 (3), pp.303-15

Callenbach, E. (1981) *Ecotopia Emerging*, Berkeley CA, Banyan Tree Books

Cantril, H. (1965) *The Pattern of Human Concerns*, New Brunswick NJ, Rutgers University Press

Clarke, I.F. (1992) 20th century future-think: all our yesterdays, *Futures*, 24 (3), pp.251-60

Chomsky, N. (1993) *Year 501: The Conquest Continues*, London, Verso

Commission for the Future (1989) *Perspectives on Australia's Future*, Paris, UNESCO

Danziger, K. (1963) Ideology and utopia in South Africa: a methodological contribution to the sociology of knowledge, *British Journal of Sociology*, vol. 14, pp.59-76

Dator, J. (1994) What is (and what is not) Futures Studies, *Papers de Prospectiva*, 1, May, Centre Catala de Prospectiva

Dixon, B. (1990) *Playing Them False: Children's Games, Toys and Puzzles*, Stoke-on-Trent, Trentham Books

Dodds, J. and Lin, C. (1992) Chinese teenagers' concerns about the future: a cross-national comparison, *Adolescence*, 27 (106), pp.481-86

Eckersley, R. (1994) A machine at the heart of the world: youth and the future. Paper for forum 'Shaping Schools Futures,' Melbourne, Vic.

Educators for Social Responsibility (1982) *Dialogue: A Teaching Guide to Nuclear Issues*, ESR, Cambridge MA

Eisler, R. (1990) *The Chalice and the Blade: Our History, Our Future*, London, Unwin Hyman

Elgin, D. (1991) Creating a sustainable future, *ReVision*, 14 (2), pp.77-79

Fien, J. (1993a) *Education for the Environment: Critical Curriculum Theorising and Environmental Education*, Geelong, Deakin University Press

Fien, J. ed. (1993b) *Teaching for a Sustainable World,* Brisbane, Australian Association for Environmental Education

Fien, J. and Gerber, R. eds. (1988) *Teaching Geography for a Better World*, Edinburgh, Oliver and Boyd

Fisher, S. and Hicks, D. (1985) *World Studies 8-13: A Teacher's Handbook*, Harlow, Oliver and Boyd

Fitch, R. and Svengalis, C. (1979) *Futures Unlimited: Teaching About Worlds to Come*, Washington DC, National Council for the Social Studies

Freeman, C. and Jahoda, M. (1978) *World Futures: The Great Debate*, Oxford, Martin Robertson

Fortunati, V. (1993) 'The metamorphosis of the apocalyptic myth: from utopia to science fiction', chapter 6 in: Kumar, K. and Bann, S. eds. *Utopias and the Millennium*, London, Reaktion Books

Galbraith, P. (1994) Futures Committee Report, Board of Senior Secondary School Studies, Queensland

Galeano, E. (1991) *The Book of Embraces*, New York, W.W. Norton

Galtung, J. (1976) 'The future: a forgotton dimension', in: Ornauer, H., Wiberg, H., Sicinski, A., and Galtung, J. eds. *Images of the World in the Year 2000*, Atlantic Highlands NJ, Humanities Press

Giddens, A. (1990) *The Consequences of Modernity*, Cambridge Polity Press

Giddens, A. (1994) *Beyond Left and Right: the Future of Radical Politics*, Cambridge, Polity Press

Gillespie, J. and Allport, G. (1955) *Youth's Outlook on the Future: A Cross-National Study*, New York, Doubleday and Co.

Goodwin, B. and Taylor, K. (1982) *The Politics of Utopia: A Study in Theory and Practice*, London, Hutchinson

Gough, N. (1988a) Futures in Australian education: tacit, token and taken for granted, *Futures*, 22 (3), pp.298-310

Gough, N. (1988b) Children's images of the future: their meaning and their implications for school curriculum, *Curriculum Concerns*, 5 (2), pp.6-10

Haas, J. (1988) *Future Studies in the K-12 Curriculum*, Boulder, Social Science Education Consortium

Harding, S. (1991) *Whose Science? Whose Knowledge? Thinking from Women's Lives*, Milton Keynes, Open University Press

Henley Centre (1991) *Young Eyes: Children's Vision of the Future Environment*, London, Henley Centre for Forecasting

Hicks, D. (1990) World Studies 8-13: a short history, *Westminster Studies in Education*, vol. 13, pp.61-80

Hicks, D. (1993a) Mapping the future: a geographical contribution, *Teaching Geography*, 18 (4), pp.146-49

Hicks, D. (1993b) Reclaiming the future: what every educator needs to know, *Australian Journal of Environmental Education*, vol. 9, pp.71-84

Hicks, D. (1994a) *Educating for the Future: A Practical Classroom Guide*, Godalming, World Wide Fund for Nature UK

Hicks, D. (1994b) *Preparing for the Future: Notes and Queries for Concerned Educators*, London, Adamantine Press

Hicks, D. and Holden, C. (1995) Exploring the future: the missing dimension in environmental education, *Environmental Education Research*, 1 (2), pp.185-93

Hicks, D. and Steiner, M. eds. (1988) *Making Global Connections: A World Studies Workbook*, Edinburgh, Oliver and Boyd

HMI (1989) *The Teaching and Learning of History and Geography*, London, HMSO

Holbrook, A. (1992) Teachers with vision and visions of teaching: the role of futures study and research in postgraduate teacher education, *Futures Research Quarterly*, 8 (4), pp.27-48

Holden, C. (1989) Teaching about the future with young children, in: Slaughter, R. ed. *Studying the Future: An Introductory Reader*, Commission for the Future and Australian Bicentennial Authority

Holden, C. and Smith, E. (1993) Economic and industrial understanding in primary education: problems and possibilities, *Education and Training*, 34 (3), pp.11-14

Huber, B. (1978) Images of the future, in: Fowles, J. ed. *Handbook of Futures Research*, Westport CT, Greenwood Press

Hughes, B. (1985) *World Futures: A Critical Analysis of Alternatives*, Baltimore, John Hopkins University Press

Hutchinson, F. (1992) *Futures Consciousness and the School: Explorations of Broad and Narrow Literacies for the Twenty-First Century with Particular Reference to Australian Young People*, PhD thesis, Armidale, University of New England

Hutchinson, F. (1993) Educating beyond fatalism and impoverished social imagination: are we actively listening to young people's voices on the future? *Peace, Environment and Education*, 4 (4), pp.36-57

Hutchinson, F. (1994) Educating beyond violent futures in children's media, *Futures*, 26 (1), pp.5-23

Hyland, T. (1991) Citizenship education and the enterprise culture, *Forum*, 33 (3)

Inayatullah, S. (1993) From 'Who am I?' to 'When am I?' *Futures*, 25 (3), pp.235-53

Independent, The (1994) 'Britain's future should be seen and not heard' and 'Youth survey shows urge for closer ties with Europe,' Monday 11th July

IUCN/UNEP/WWF (1991) *Caring for the Earth: A Strategy for Sustainable Living*, London, Earthscan Publications

Johnson, L. (1987) Children's visions of the future, *The Futurist*, 21 (3), pp.36-40

Jungk, R. and Mullert, N. (1987) *Future Workshops: How to Create Desirable Futures*, London, Institute for Social Inventions

Keepin, W. (1991) Toward an ecological psychology, *ReVision*, 14, pp.90-100

Kleiber, D., Major, W. and Manaster, G. (1993) Youth's outlook on the future IV: a third past-present comparison, *Youth and Society*, 24 (4), pp.349-62

Kumar, K. (1991) *Utopianism*, Milton Keynes, Open University Press

Kumar, K. (1993) The end of socialism? The end of utopia? The end of history? chapter 5 in: Kumar, K. and Bann, S. eds. *Utopias and the Millennium*, London, Reaktion Books

Lefanu, S. (1988) *In the Chinks of the World Machine: Feminism and Science Fiction*, London, The Women's Press

Levitas, R. (1990) *The Concept of Utopia*, Hemel Hempstead, Philip Allan

Lister, I. (1987) Global and international approaches to political education, in: Lister, I. ed. *Political Education in Britain*, London, Falmer Press

Livingstone, D. (1976) Images of the educational future in advanced industrial society: an Ontario enquiry, *Canadian Journal of Education*, 1 (2), pp.13-29

Livingstone, D. (1983) Intellectual and popular images of the educational and social future, in *Class Ideologies and Educational Futures*, London, Falmer Press

Mac an Ghaill, M. (1994) *The Making of Men*, Buckingham, Open University Press

Marien, M. (1985) Toward a new futures research: insights from twelve types of futurists, *Futures Research Quarterly*, 1 (1), pp.13-33

Marien, M. (1992) Environmental problems and sustainable futures, *Futures*, 24 (8), pp.731-58

Marien, M. (1994) *Futures Survey Annual 1994*, Bethesda MA, World Future Society

Masini, E. (1987) Women as builders of the future, *Futures*, August, pp.431-36

Masser, I. et al (1992) *The Geography of Europe's Futures*, Belhaven, London Press

McLaughlin, C. and Davidson, G. (1985) *Builders of the Dawn: Community Lifestyles in a Changing World*, Summertown TN, Book Publishing Company

Meadows, D. and D., Randers, J. and Behrens, W. (1972) *The Limits to Growth*, London, Earth Island

Meadows, D., Meadows, D. and Randers, J. (1993) *Beyond the Limits: Global Collapse or Sustainable Future*, London, Earthscan Publications

Merchant, C. (1992) *Radical Ecology: The Search for a Livable World*, London, Routledge

Milbrath, L. (1989) *Envisioning a Sustainable Society: Learning Our Way Out*, Albany, State University of New York

Moll, P. (1991) *From Scarcity to Sustainability. Futures Studies and the Environment: The Role of the Club of Rome*, Frankfurt, Peter Lang

Ornauer, H., Wiberg, H., Sicinski, A., and Galtung, J. eds. (1976) *Images of the World in the Year 2000*, Atlantic Highlands NJ, Humanities Press

O'Rourke, B. (1994) 'Futures and the curriculum', chapter in: *Shaping the Future: Review of the Queensland School Curriculum*, vol. 3, State of Queensland, Brisbane

Orr, D. (1992) *Ecological Literacy: Education and the Transition to a Postmodern World*, Albany, State University of New York Press

Orr, D. (1993) Schools for the twenty-first century, *Resurgence*, September/October, No. 160, pp.16-19

Piercy, M. (1976) *Woman on the Edge of Time*, London, Women's Press

Pike, G. and Selby, D. (1988) *Global Teacher, Global Learner*, London, Hodder and Stoughton

Pike, G. and Selby, D. (1995) *Reconnecting: From National to Global Curriculum*, Godalming, World Wide Fund for Nature UK

Polak, F. (1972) *The Image of the Future* (E. Boulding, Trans. and Abr.), San Francisco, Jossey-Bass/Elsevier. (Original work published 1955)

Postel, S. (1992) Denial in the decisive decade, chapter 1 in: *State of the World 1992*, Worldwatch Institute, London, Earthscan Publications

Public Voice International (1994) *Choices for Britain: Avon Pilot Evaluation*, Bristol

Richardson, R. (1990) *Daring to be a Teacher: Essays, Stories and Memoranda*, Stoke-on-Trent, Trentham Books

Riley, K. (1989) *Toward Tomorrow*, New York, Scholastic Inc.

Rundall, K. (1994) Personal communication to the author

Saferworld (1993a) *Choices for Britain: Teacher's Guide*, Bristol

Saferworld (1993b) *Choices for Britain: It's Your Future*, Bristol

Said, E. (1993) *Culture and Imperialism*, London, Vintage

Sardar, Z. (1993) Do not adjust your mind: post-modernism, reality and the Other, *Futures*, 25 (8), pp.877-893

Scott, A. (1992) 'Political culture and social movements', chapter 3 in: *Political and Economic Forms of Modernity*, Allen, J., Braham, P., and Lewis, P. eds., Cambridge, Polity Press

Shiva, V. (1989) *Staying Alive: Women, Ecology and Development*, London, Zed Books

Slaughter, R. (1993) Futures concepts, *Futures*, 25 (3), pp.289-314

Slaughter, R. (1994) Draft outline for *Futures: Personal, Social and Global*, University of Melbourne

Slaughter, R. (1995) *The Foresight Principle*, London, Adamantine Press

Smith, G.A. (1992) *Education and the Environment: Learning to Live with Limits*, Albany, State University of New York Press

Starhawk (1994) *The Fifth Sacred Thing*, HarperSanFrancisco

Steiner, M. ed. (1995) *Developing the Global Teacher: Theory to Practice in Teacher Education*, Stoke-on-Trent, Trentham Books

Toffler, A. (1974) *Learning for Tomorrow: The Role of the Future in Education*, New York, Vintage Books

Wagar, W. (1992) *The Next Three Futures: Paradigms of Things to Come*, London, Adamantine Press

Weekly Reader (1993) *The Weekly Reader National Survey on the Future*, Middletown CT, Weekly Reader Corporation

Weigand, P. (1995) Geography, in: Anning, A. ed. *The National Curriculum Five Years On*, Buckingham, Open University Press

Weiss, E.B. (1989) *In Fairness to Future Generations*, New York, Transnational Publishers

Whaley, C. and H. (1986) *Future Images: Futures Studies for Grades 4 to 12*, New York, Trillium Press

Whitaker, P. (1995) *Managing to Learn: Aspects of Reflective and Experiential Learning in Schools*, London, Cassell

Wiltshire, K. et al. (1994) *Review of the Queensland School Curriculum*, vol. 1, State of Queensland, Brisbane

Ziegler, W. (1989) *Envisioning the Future: A Mindbook of Exercises for Futures-Inventors*, Denver, Futures-Invention Associates

Ziegler, R. (1991) Envisioning the future, *Futures*, 23 (5), pp.516-527

Index

155